40 Perfect New York Days

40 Perfect New York Days

Walks and Rambles
In and Around the City

Joan Gregg
Serena Nanda
Beth Pacheco

iUniverse Star
New York Lincoln Shanghai

40 Perfect New York Days
Walks and Rambles In and Around the City

iUniverse Star
an iUniverse, Inc. imprint

For information address:
iUniverse, Inc.
2021 Pine Lake Road, Suite 100
Lincoln, NE 68512
www.iuniverse.com

ISBN: 0-595-29742-0

Printed in the United States of America

The authors and iUniverse have done our best to provide current and precise information. Please check maps, telephone numbers and walking distances to avoid disappointments and sore feet.

Dedicated to
"The Ancient, Renowned and Delectable City of Gotham"

Washington Irving,
Knickerbocker's History of New York (1809)

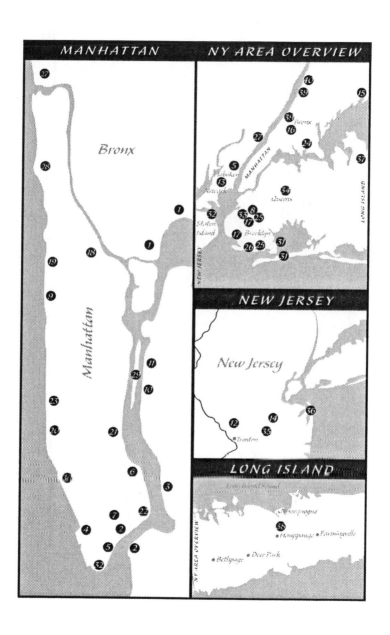

Contents

Past and Present

Bridging the Past, Bridging the Boroughs 3

Jumel Mansion, the Macombs Dam Bridge Walk to Yankee Stadium and the Art Deco Grand Concourse to the Bronx Museum

> George Washington really did sleep in the Jumel Mansion and Wilt "the stilt" Chamberlain did get his start in Harlem's Rucker Playground! All this plus the grandest boulevard in the Bronx and a new perspective on this overlooked borough. And maybe a ballgame at the "house that Ruth built."

Brooklyn Beauties 7

The Great Bridge and Historic Brooklyn Heights

> Today's walk takes you across the Brooklyn Bridge, a splendid New York icon, and into Brooklyn Heights, the city's best preserved brownstone neighborhood and its first historic landmark district. And the best ice cream in the world!

Art, Funk and Cultural Diversity in Brooklyn 15

Walking Williamsburg and Historic Greenpoint

> Even as an 18th century rural outpost, this part of Brooklyn was a center of diversity. With the march of industry, it became even more so. Today, its distinctive architecture and cultural diversity is enhanced by artists and new waves of immigrants, who have added funky and authentic ethnic shops and restaurants.

This moderate-length walk packs in the history of the city's oldest section with reminders of colonial conviviality, heroic deeds and new insights on the "father of our country." See how lower Manhattan is rebuilding after the tragedy of 9-11.

This cross-Hudson excursion includes stellar exhibits of Native American culture, a Hudson River ferry ride and spectacular views of the city from the heights of Hoboken (with an Italian pastry at Frank Sinatra's favorite bakery to sweeten the day.)

Salute the "transit trade" and "carriage trade"-the ladies (and gents) who marched for the vote and a decent wage and who waltzed in the splendid ballrooms of Gramercy Park. Exceptional galleries and the "most beautiful block" in New York complete the day.

Enjoy ethnic art, food, and shopping as you follow in the footprints of the immigrants who have made our city great. African slaves and freemen, Europeans of many backgrounds and a diversity of Asians have all contributed to Lower Manhattan, an area that can't be duplicated anywhere in the world.

Truth and Beauty

The Brooklyn Museum, whose ecclectic holdings rival the great European collections, borders an urban paradise, the Brooklyn Botanic Gardens. No passport or visa required: a Metrocard transports you here for a richly varied day.

Spiritual treasures abound on this Upper West Side excursion. Hear the bells in Riverside Church and experience the great Cathedral Church of St. John the Divine. After breaking bread in the West Side manner, encounter a Russian mystic's multi-faceted legacy in a townhouse museum.

The #7 local takes you to Queens for a day of fine, folk, fauve and fresh art in a factory, a warehouse, and a public school transformed into gallery space. Lunch in Queens is ethnic, ethnic or ethnic.

This multicultural day in Queens combines striking sculpture in unique settings, spectacular Manhattan views and mouth watering ethnic food.

A short train ride takes you to the famous university's beautiful campus to discover its rich art collections and neo-gothic architecture. Lunch with the ivy leaguers on or off campus and visit the shops and landmark buildings near historic Palmer Square.

It's not the yellow brick road, but PATH leads you to a world-class museum, a Portuguese neighborhood with authentic ethnic food and ALL THAT JAZZ at a special brunch. In season, there is a glorious Cherry Blossom walk.

Another great day in the Garden State, accessible by train or car, combines the outdoors and indoors for a lovely nature walk, garden display and a most unusual collection of dissident Soviet art.

City Beats

> From the Flatiron Building at Fifth Avenue, across Chelsea to the
> river, today's walk includes a fabulous fashion museum, the
> Victorian Hotel Chelsea, whose lobby features the creativity of its
> many resident artists, and the DIA Center for the Arts. Then wind
> up and unwind at Chelsea Piers.

> World-shaking ideas in commerce, theatre, international relations,
> knowledge, and architecture are enshsrined on 42nd St., the great
> heart of New York City. You'll experience them all in this river to
> river walk which includes Grand Central Terminal, the Chrysler
> Building, the United Nations, the New York Public Library and
> Times Square.

> This grand loop embraces the East River's lovely waterside path, the
> East Village, the Lower East Side's remarkable Tenement Museum,
> discount shopping and a Chinese foot massage.

> Today's perfect walk takes you on and near Fifth Avenue into New
> York's quiet, brilliant gems: The ICP, where pictures say more than
> words, a public library in a marble Beaux Arts "temple," our largest
> cathedral and the Dahesh Museum: a space for art with grace. At
> day's end, rest beside New York City's highest waterfall.

On the Waterfront

> Gorgeous greenery, an historic mansion and super seafood with a
> view await you on this great amble (or bike ride) in the upper Bronx.

>   That's Buckingham Place, not Palace-a hidden neighborhood of
>   19th century homes and centuries old trees. A hop on the subway
>   takes you on to Brooklyn's boat-filled Sheepshead Bay and a swim
>   (in season) at the city's most tranquil beach (with a great playground
>   for kids nearby).

>   Experience the transformations of these historic ocean-front resorts
>   that have spelled fun and fantasy for generations of New Yorkers.
>   Enjoy classic Italian or authentic Russian food, or even that old
>   favorite, a Nathan's hotdog. Go in January for a swim with the Polar
>   Bears.

>   This delightful 2-5 mile walk combines unparalleled views of the
>   majestic Hudson River and city skyline from one of the world's most
>   beautiful bridges, atop the Palisades and along the riverbank. In
>   Winter you can smell the roses!

>   Hike the forest wilderness of Inwood Park and you won't believe
>   you're still in the city. But you'll know you are, when you eat deli-
>   cious ethnic food in Washington Heights. Then head down to the
>   Cloisters Museum, with its Hudson River views and the famous
>   Unicorn Tapestries.

>   A visit to Southeby's Auction House and the charming Mt. Vernon
>   Hotel and Garden takes you back to New York's olden days. The
>   Tram ride to Roosevelt Island introduces you to a successful modern
>   experiment in urban living and glorious river views.

This unique pathway along New York's two rivers, with a baker's dozen of diversions, is a magnet for walkers and bikers. Take your pick of the Chelsea Market, a shipboard military museum, lunch on the Hudson or all of the above.

Enjoy two beautiful seascapes on this all-season nature-lover's excursion. Binoculars, a camera and a metrocard are all you need to visit New York City's largest bird sanctuary and one of our finest beach parks.

This unforgettable excursion in the city's "fifth borough" offers the magnificent Manhattan skyline by day and by night from the ferry; a riverside path; and the other-worldly loveliness of a Ming Dynasty Scholar's Garden. A ballgame in Staten Island's Yankee "stadium with a view" or a dinner with live jazz ends the day.

Great Escapes

Take your choice of outdoor pleasures in the Park-hike, bike, jog, ski, picnic, even drum. Meander through a child-friendly zoo or listen to classical music under the stars. Continue to nearby Park Slope, an historic district of beautiful brownstones and broad avenues lined with shops, pubs, and appealing restaurants.

You can see the forest for the trees on this sylvan stroll through one of New York's most exclusive neighborhoods and along park trails tranquil in any season. Extend your day with an ethnic dinner or a classic hot fudge sundae in a setting from the funky fifties.

This divine botanical garden with sculptures inspired by myth, poetry, painting, drama and dance is a treat for the senses and a revitalizing experience for mind, body and soul. By car or train, it's worth the hour long ride.

Take an unforgettable ferry ride under the spectacular Verrazano Bridge to the Gateway National Seashore for unspoiled beaches (in the buff if you like) with views of the lower Manhattan skyline.

A glorious day of art indoors and out, hidden away on Long Island's gold coast, an easy trip from the city. If you're driving, search out the charming restaurants on the waterfront at near-by Long Island towns.

Canoe or kayak this beautiful placid river to Long Island Sound. Spring and Summer will awe you (and the children) with greenery and birdlife. Fall delights with spectacular changing colors on this journey through one of the last undeveloped spots on Long Island.

Amble along the converted "Old Put" railroad line, brunch or lunch with beautiful Hudson views and browse through the Red Grooms bookstore-unlike any you've ever seen-at the Hudson River Museum in Westchester. A coffee at gorgeous Wave Hill in Riverdale tops off this special day.

A pretty lake walk in the Rockefeller Preserve, lunch in charming Tarrytown, and visits to a unique art-filled church and a nearby historic home is a triple treat just a half hour north of the city.

For their assistance, encouragement and companionship, our thanks to the following people:

Anita Aboulafia, Mike Altman, Fred and Bianca Baar, Barbara Backer, Judith Barbanel and Jerry Sieser, Santo Berenato, Fern Bodner, Abby Bond, Steve Brewer, Ruth Britton, Jasper Burns, Carole and Ron Busch, Audrey Cody, Gloria Cornejo, Jeanne Dyer, Sue and Al Engel, Lottie Feinberg, Paulette Forbes-Igharo, Edward J. Fortier, Marty Fromm, Sheryl Fullerton, Ora and Myron Gelberg, Sy Goldman, Paisley Gregg, Andrea Herman, Denise Hetz, Jane Hoffer, Jim Horelick, Emily and Ed Hyans, Linda John, Nina Kalen, Jim and Diane Kelly, Richard Kenefick, Ray Kennedy, Alla Khramova, Sara Kramer, Lillian Kristal, Joan Kutner, Carrol Lasker, Joan Levinson, Tom Litwack, Harriet Luria, Gregory Mack, Steve Margolis, Ram and Santosh Mehta, Elizabeth and Floyd Miller, Monty Mitchell, Saiko Mori, Jai and Kathleen Nanda, Raj, Helena, Alexander and Adriana Nanda, Robin Nanda, Judy Nazario and the people in the John Jay College Computer Technology Dept., Jill Norgren, Edward J. Fortier, Russell Oberlin, Sharon Oliensis, Marcos Pacheco and Jennifer Stefancin, Pat Parks, Bill Pennell, Steve Reichstein, John and Richanda Rhoden, Rita Rosenkranz, Larry and Linda Rubin, Joan and Alfred Russell, Rekha Schoumaker, Dennis Sherman, Fred Steinberg, Tom Steinberg, Timothy Stevens, Charles Stickney, Jeff Talan, Peggy Taub, Ric Turer, Gwen Thompson, Zelda Warner, Eric Watts, Mary Winslow and Michael Keenan, Jane Wolff, Kathy Wylde

Another Perfect Day,
Gimme a Break

Bart Simpson

Forty Perfect New York Days is meant to be your personal companion in and around the city, a knowledgeable friend suggesting offbeat, upbeat places to visit that provide unique and intimate encounters with the world's most exciting urban landscape. We're three New Yorkers who've lived, worked, played and raised our children here. As New Yorkers we're walkers: we stroll the city streets and the boardwalks, visit the museums and the galleries and hike the paths of surprising beauty in all five boroughs and beyond. We ride the ferries, the busses and the subways and cycle the bikepaths. We dine in the city's cafes and restaurants, enjoy its cultural performances, dance on its piers and swim at its beaches. Each Day in our guide has been tried and tested not once, but many times over the years. So we've been there, loved it and want to share it.

    Forty Perfect New York Days offers new adventures of an urban kind and convenient rambles into nature for active, curious New Yorkers and visitors. Our Days celebrate New York's legendary diversity of places, people and things to see and do, taking you to upbeat, offbeat neighborhoods and the nooks and crannies of all 5 boroughs and nearby towns, beaches and gardens.

    The format of **Forty Perfect New York Days** takes the stress out of enjoying the city and its surroundings. The Days' commentaries give you a new perspective on familiar sites and interesting historical detail about lesser-known locations. Each Day's plan guides you along the best routes for the attractions of the locale, but the routes are flexible enough to allow for personal discoveries and individualized time frames. The Days are moderately paced (and moderately priced), and include snack breaks and luncheon suggestions in tune with the ambiance of the journey. Most Days are accessible by public transportation. Precise, easy-to-follow directions get you there and back, in and around, with a minimum of fuss. The annotated Table of Contents encourages spontaneous choices for a Day, depending on the weather, your mood and your company.

An Orientation, useful Appendices to New York City Information and a Special Events Calendar help you make the most of the city and environs. So go to the Table of Contents, select a perfect day, and get moving. You'll find that when we say "Have a Great Day!" we really mean it and we make it happen.

Authors' Note

On September 10, 2001, we had just finished the outline for this book. On September 11, we witnessed the attacks on the Twin Towers from our nearby neighborhoods. Shocked and devastated in spirit, as were all New Yorkers, indeed all Americans, we contemplated the ruins and grieved for the loss of so many innocent lives. We agreed to put our project away. How could we revisit our "perfect days" of the past when the streets of every neighborhood were now filled with shrines of flowers, candles, photographs and messages of sorrow? So much of the the city we love had been damaged, disrupted and destroyed—its morale as well as its more concrete icons.

But New York is a city that has risen phoenix-like many times in its history, and New Yorkers now, as many times in the past, showed a determination to "get back to normal" that made sense to us. We saw a recommittment to our project as a recommittment to the city. It would not be the same New York that we had initially mapped out, but change has been the hallmark of New York since its earliest days. We were certain that New York would continue to cast its spell—over its devoted residents and visitors alike—as the world's greatest modern city.

Orientation

Whether you're a New Yorker who knows your own neighborhood blindfolded, a recent arrival to the city, a tourist here for an extended stay or a return visitor, these practical suggestions will help you make the most of 40 Perfect New York Days.

Look through the entire Day before setting out. Although most days can be done at the spur of the moment, a few days do require advance reservations. **Always telephone ahead** to check a particular site, restaurant or exhibit to avoid disappointment. Most Days begin around 10AM and end around 4PM. Transportation is calculated from midtown Manhattan; most sites can be reached in under an hour. Walking distances are generally less than 3.5 miles (and flat).

Consult the **Special Events Appendix,** arranged by month, to incorporate a special happening related to your Day. If you only have one day in New York and have not been here before, see the **One Perfect Day Appendix.**

Each Day provides clear transportation and walking directions to, from, and along your route. Along with **40 Perfect New York Days**, it is also useful to take a relevant **subway and bus map** (obtainable at most subway stations. Transportation maps for the entire city are available at the main MTA Center upstairs at the Jay St./Borough Hall Brooklyn subway station). Main city tourist offices, listed in our **Appendix Want To Know More?** also provide maps. The **MTA Travel Information Center, 1-718-330-1234,** offers the most current subway and bus information.

City street, neighborhood and area focus maps are available at city information agencies listed in the **Appendix Want To Know More;** listed websites may also supply detailed maps. The large neighborhood maps on the walls of most subway stations are also useful. Park Visitor Centers and Museum Information counters also supply useful material for getting around their sites.

Public Transportation is the best way to reach the sites described on most of our Days. Where a car is necessary, it is so noted, with driving directions. **Discount Metrocards** are available at subway vending machines; you can pay with cash, ATM or credit card. Regular Metrocards are also available at token booths. Metrocards offer free transfer between 2 busses in any direction or between subway and bus (but not from bus to subway) within 2 hours. If you're using a train beyond the city borders, you may find it useful to pick up your ticket–and a return schedule–in advance.

Cruising yellow, metered **taxicabs** take up to 4 people. A tip of 15% of the final fare is reasonable for a satisfactory ride. Fares are posted on the door.

Bicycles are not permitted on city sidewalks; they may be taken on subway, PATH lines and ferries except at rush hour. Always wear a helmet.

Most **restaurants** take credit cards, but some smaller one (and many in Chinatown) don't. Call ahead or be prepared to pay cash. A reasonable tip for satisfactory service is 15–18%.

Past and Present

WALKING MAP

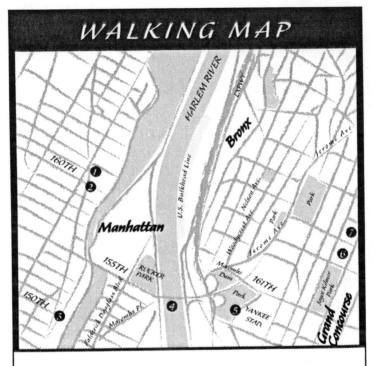

- **❶** Jumel Mansion
- **❷** Sylvan Terrace
- **❸** Bailey Blake House
- **❹** Macombs Dam Bridge
- **❺** Yankee Stadium
- **❻** Grand Concourse
- **❼** Bronx Museum

Bridging the Past,
Bridging the Boroughs

Jumel Mansion, the Macombs Dam Bridge Walk to Yankee Stadium and the Art Deco Grand Concourse to the Bronx Museum

While the sites on this perfect "borough to borough" day are all worth doing individually, stacking them up on this surprisingly moderate walk gives you a fascinating "borough to borough" perspective on our city. From **Harlem's Morris-Jumel Mansion**, Manhattan's only remaining Colonial residence, it's under a mile down neighborly St. Nicholas Ave. and across the Harlem River on the **Macombs Dam Bridge**, a fine 19th century swing bridge. On the Bronx side, America's best **Art Deco-Art Moderne facades** outside of Miami Beach await you on the **Grand Concourse**. That famous boulevard also houses the innovative **Bronx Museum**, whose "living" exhibits have included a complete Bronx beauty parlor.

To reach the mid-18th century **Jumel Mansion** (65 Jumel Terrace at 160th Street; 1-212-923-8008; W-Sun 10–4PM; $3 [call for Urban Ranger guided tours and special programs]), take the C train to the 163/Edgecombe Ave. station. George Washington really did sleep in this unique historical home, which served as military headquarters for the "father of our country" and hosted many of our Revolution's most important figures. Don't miss the architectural delight of **Sylvan Terrace**, two rows of tiny, late 19th century clapboard houses on a cobblestoned street just across the way from the Mansion.

Leave the Museum for the **Macombs Dam Bridge** at 155th St. and walk down **St. Nicholas Avenue**, with its grand, pre-war apartment houses and the family-friendly atmosphere of a traditional New York neighborhood. Fans of Victorian architecture may want to take a short diversion to 150th St. and St. Nicholas Place for the whimsical, turreted 1888 **Bailey-Blake House**, built by the circus entrepreneur James Baily, but now owned by Mr. and Mrs. Blake (the latter a Cotton Club dancer's daughter who grew up here.)

The pedestrian entrance to the **Macombs Dam Bridge** is on 155th St.; stay on your left hand side to view the Polo Grounds housing project below, built on the site of the former NY Giants baseball stadium, where Bobby Thompson hit the "home run heard round the world." Also visible below is the famed **Holcombe Rucker Basketball Playground**, which produced such basketball greats as Wilt "the stilt" Chamberlain and Kareem Abdul-Jabar. Named for the neighborhood resident who began an "each one teach one" basketball program linked to educational improvement, the playground hosts a fabulous summer basketball tournament when many court greats return for a game (see Special Events, August). Cross over to the Bridge's south side—a sign midway through announces "**The Bronx**"—and continue to the end of the pedestrian path.

Hungry? Where the Bridge walkway ends, a right turn takes you to the undistinguished looking building of the **Flash Inn**, a venerable Italian restaurant frequented by Yankee ballplayers, high roller fans, politicos and other cognoscenti (107 Macombs Place; 1-212-283-8605; M-Th 11AM-late; F, Sat, Sun 2PM-late). The **Yankee Stadium**, "the house that Ruth built" is ahead on your left. For a good diner lunch, keep on the walkway past Yankee Stadium itself to the blue fence (do NOT turn right or you'll hit the highway), continue to 161st Street past the Lexington Ave. elevated subway and walk up one block to **Unity**

Coffee Shop (64 161st St.); there's excellent bakery takeout next door at Stadium Bake Shop (#66).

Continue your walk up 161st St. to Joyce Kilmer Park, whose 1899 Lorelei Fountain statue of Heinrich Heine was donated by the community's then German-Jewish residents because the city rejected a more prominent Manhattan location for the statue of a foreigner and a Jew. At the **Grand Concourse**, a left turn takes you to the Bronx Museum past some of the fine **Art Deco, Art Moderne and Modernist buildings** that continue up into the 170s and onto some of the side streets. At 851 161st St. is the **Bronx County Building**, a Moderne limestone tower with sleek sculptures and friezes; at 1125 is the French-inspired garden-set **Andrew Freedman Home** (for the Aged); at 167th St., #s 1150, 1166 and 1188 are typical 1930s apartment houses with Art Deco and Art Moderne embellishments such as sawtooth brick and mosaics. The **Bronx Museum** (1040 Grand Concourse/165th St.; 1-718-681-6000; W 12–9 free; Th-Sun 12-6; suggested adm. $3–5) is itself interestingly housed in a 1960s synagogue.

Directions To Jumel Mansion take the back end of C train to the 163rd Street station, ascend stairs on the left, pass the supermarket and climb the steps to the long stone wall. Macombs Dam Bridge is accessed by the same subway at the 155th St. station. To access the Yankee Stadium-Grand Concourse-Bronx Museum part of the day, take the Lexington Ave. #4 or B/D train to 161st St.

Want to Know More? The Jumel Mansion website: www.morisjumel.org Documentary videos about the Rucker Playground are "On Hallowed Ground: Streetball Champions of Rucker Park" and "On the Rim." For books about the Bronx see The Unbeatable Bronx Day. For Yankee Stadium see "Yankee Stadium: 75 Years of Drama, Glamour and Glory," Ray Robinson and Christopher Jennison (1998)

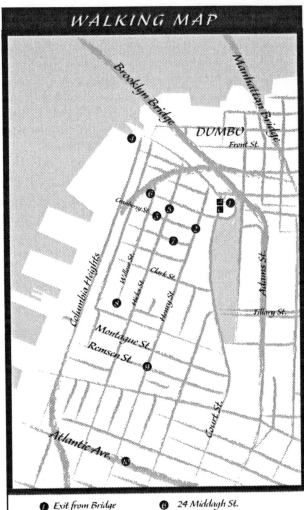

WALKING MAP

DUMBO

Front St.

Brooklyn Bridge

Manhattan Bridge

Cranberry St.

Columbia Heights

Willow St.

Hicks St.

Clark St.

Henry St.

Adams St.

Tillary St.

Montague St.

Remsen St.

Court St.

Atlantic Ave.

1	Exit from Bridge	6	24 Middagh St.
2	Entrance to Heights	7	Plymouth Church
3	19 Cranberry St.	8	70 Willow
4	Ferry Bank	9	84 Remsen
5	50 Hicks and Kids	10	Sahadi

Brooklyn Beauties

The Great Bridge
and Historic Brooklyn Heights

This perfect day begins with a walk across **the Brooklyn Bridge.**
The Bridge has been portrayed in literature and all of the visual
arts. Yet, no poem, no painting, postcard, or photograph has ever
captured its perfect design and the splendor of New York Harbor
which it spans. The excursion continues through **Brooklyn
Heights,** a living museum of Americana with fine architecture,
historical sites and beautiful views. Farms were not subdivided
into city blocks here until 1814, when Robert Fulton's steam
driven ferry opened the area to settlement by affluent Wall
Streeters, eager to commute to Brooklyn's pleasant "suburb."
(Some things never change.) There are many opportunities for
dining and simply enjoying the unique ambience. After a walk
from the Bridge through the **North Heights** onto the sublime
Promenade, we suggest three possible routes. Visitors may decide
to cover them all or to defer one or two for a return visit.

   **The first route is along the Promenade, exiting at Montague
St., a bustling shopping street. It continues** to **Atlantic Avenue,**
the Heights' southern border, which is the commercial center of
Brooklyn's Arabic community and a stretch of antique shops,
boutiques and good restaurants. **Route 2 is north and downhill
to the historic Ferry Bank District, below the "heights" on the
waterfront.** The view here is choice, as is the fresh ice cream,
after 1 PM. Nearby is **DUMBO** (down under the Manhattan
Bridge), New York's latest emerging neighborhood for loft-living,

galleries, a chocolate factory, specialty shops, and restaurants. **Route 3, "Willow Street, Turning a Few Corners" is a walking tour** that covers several blocks, detailing the features of austere Federal row houses and the later, increasingly more ornate brownstone revivals; it too concludes on **Atlantic Avenue.**

Begin today's excursion at the Brooklyn Bridge in front of the Municipal Building on Center Street, Manhattan at the #4/5/6 stop of the Brooklyn Bridge subway station. Note the symbols designating the walking path and the bike path. The Bridge is an architectural triumph, but its construction was marked by tragedy. Architect John A. Roebling died of injuries sustained as building began. He was replaced by his son, Washington, who contracted debilitating bends while inspecting one of the giant caissons. The younger Roebling's unofficial second in command was his wife, Emily. From their home on Columbia Heights, the couple monitored progress through a spyglass. Mrs. Roebling carried instructions to workers and represented her husband in political and fund raising activities. A plaque on the south end of the bridge honors Emily Roebling, 19th century style: *"Back of every great work we can find the self sacrificing devotion of a woman."*

The Bridge is 1.3 miles. The central span, suspended by cables, is 1,595 feet long. Bronze tablets beneath the cathedral-like arches depict stages in construction and identify sites in the harbor. Look back towards Manhattan to see juxtaposed images of several centuries: 20th century skyscrapers; 19th century delicately twisted woven steel cables and tall sailing ships anchored at South Street; 17th century blue cobblestone streets, where the first European immigrants—Dutch burghers—and the "first people," Native Americans, traded their wares. Imagine Henrik Hudson's Half Moon gliding in full sail across the waters that have borne the valiant captain's name since the 1600s.

Take the Bridge's first exit, a staircase to the left. Turn right at the foot of the stairs; walk several feet up the hill into a park on the right. Follow the park path to Cadman Plaza West. Cross

Henry St., the Height's eastern border onto **Cranberry Street.** While many streets retain the names of the original Dutch landowners, Cranberry St. is one of several "fruit streets," so named because a truculent Ms. Middagh of the esteemed Dutch Middaghs disliked the families whose names were given to these streets and replaced them with fruits. **Middagh St. is one block right.** Among the oldest streets, it has the greatest number of surviving wooden houses. One block left at 67 Orange St. is Plymouth Church of the Pilgrims, a national historic monument, whose minister during the Civil War was Henry Ward Beecher, brother of Harriet Beecher Stowe, the author of "Uncle Tom's Cabin." In a sermon, intended to dramatize the abolitionist cause, Minister Beecher auctioned off a young slave for the price of her freedom. A secret passage beneath the meeting house is where Beecher is said to have held trysts with ladies of the congregation, who were overcome by piety and the Minister's legendary charisma.

Continue west to the (1953) **Promenade at Columbia Heights.** This walkway, overarching the Brooklyn Queens Expressway, was the activist community's alternative to hacking up interior streets for the highway. Folks do promenade here, particularly on summer evenings, cooled by river breezes and entranced by the sparkling lights of a skyline that still reaches for the stars. When Abraham Lincoln visited during the Civil War, the somber President found solace here. Looking out over the water, he said, *"There may be more beautiful views in the world, but I don't believe it."* **Route 1** continues south along the Promenade. Along the way, see bronze pavement plaques, reliefs of the Harbor view in 1776, 1880, 1935 and 2000. The last, of course, indicates where the Twin Towers were positioned on the skyline. Farther south, at the Pierrepont entrance, a photograph mounted on the fence does the same. At midpoint, the turnoff to Montague St., a small park encloses the site of "Four Chimneys," Washington's headquarters. See our "Willow Street Walk" below for the continuation to Atlantic Avenue.

For Route 2, the **Ferry Bank District**, turn right on **Columbia Heights** and walk downhill to the restored pier. From this site, in 1776, the battle of Long Island was saved for the Americans when Washington's troops rowed across the East River to safety in Manhattan; note the fine revolutionary markers. Walt Whitman's evocative poetry is etched into the waterfront railing. *"I am with you men and women of a generation or ever so many generations hence. Just as you feel when you look at the river and sky, so I felt."* Whitman's momentous work, "Leaves of Grass," was printed nearby on Old Fulton St. where he was editor of the influential abolitionist newspaper "The Brooklyn Daily Eagle." The nearby Eagle Warehouse bears a memorial plaque. Continue along Front St for **DUMBO**.

Hungry Now Or Later? In the **North Heights**, a good lunch choice is **Tut Café** (47 Hicks St.). (Across the street, check out 50 Hicks and Kids for imports and original children's clothing; Pucci the cat may be asleep in his dolls bed in the window.) **Cranberry's** (40 Henry St.) has delicious take-out for enjoying on the Promenade. For dining later, try **Noodle Pudding** (38 Henry St.; **no credit cards**). The **Ferry Bank District** is home to "**glam**" **River Café** (1 Water St; 1-718-522-500). People line up around the block for N.Y.'s **#1 coal-oven pizza at Grimaldis** (19 Old Fulton). Very close in **Dumbo** are **Jacques Torres Chocolates** (66 Water St), **Rice** (81 Washington St) and **5 Front** (5 Front St). Montague St. has many restaurants and cafes: **Lassen and Hennings** (#114) has exceptional take-out. Locals like **Theresa's Polish** (#80). **Atlantic Avenue** offers many Middle Eastern restaurants. Come early for French **La Bouillabaise** (#145).

Route 3: "Willow Street Walk, Turning a Few Corners" begins at the Promenade. Retrace your steps on Cranberry St. to Willow; turn left 1 block to **#24 Middagh**, the "Queen" of Heights houses. This wood painted, gable-roofed Federal building with a connected garden cottage is praised by architects: "Proportion, rhythm, materials, and color are in concert throughout." See the last surviving willow tree in the garden.

Henry Ward Beecher lived at 22 Willow; rear porches overlook the harbor. Walk north to Cranberry/Willow Sts. Right, #s13, 15 and 19 Cranberry are Greek revivals (1829–1834). #19's add-on mansard roof indicates that as the country expanded into empire-building, the taste for classic simplicity gave way to ornamentation and ostentation. At #19 is the house where where Cher and Nicolas Cage pledged their love in the film "Moonstruck." Once a warehouse, #23 is the studio and home of artists Richanda and John Rhoden (1914–2001); John's smaller sculptures may be displayed beneath the wrought iron balcony.

Return to Willow; turn left to #s 40–47, where two daughters divided one (1860) house; a stairway is tucked into each twelve foot wide unit. At #70, Jackie Kennedy took painting lessons with Truman Capote at his sunny, yellow brick (1839) Greek revival, whose lovely garden is visible from the sidewalk. Among New York's finest examples of the Queen Anne style are #s108,110 and 112, Victorian whimsies replete with terracotta reliefs, elaborate doorways, bay windows, towers and dormers. The carriage house at #151 and the neighboring brick Federals #s155, 157 and 159 may have been safe houses for slaves escaping to Canada. Examine the ground level skylight at the iron gate of #157 to see a tunnel leading to a shared stable. These houses, set back from the street, were built to a pre-1830 town plan.

Continue to Pierrepont St., the first of several broad east-west avenues that are lined with elegant Victorian brownstones. The1857 Renaissance revival mansions at #s2 and 3 Pierrepont Place are considered the most impressive brownstones remaining in New York. The latter was a setting for the academy award winning film "Prizzi's Honor." Walking east along Pierrepont St., don't miss the extravagant 1890 Romanesque revival at #84. Built for the mistress of notorious Boss Tweed, it has also been a residence for Franciscan brothers. Turn right on Henry St.; walk one block to Montague St. for shops and restaurants. A block south is the mews, Grace Court Alley, once the stable alley for Remsen Street mansions. Off the next fine cross street,

Joralemon, you will find pretty Garden Place, Sidney Place, and Hunts Lane, another carriage house mews. These lovely streets take you to Atlantic Avenue for dining, antiques, and the famous Sahadi Arabic delicacies (#187).

Directions Begin at the #4/5/6 Brooklyn Bridge/City Hall subway stop. Return via the Brooklyn Bridge, or by the #4/5 or #2/3 trains at Brooklyn's Borough Hall Station; the #A/C train at High Street station, or the #2/3 stop at Clark Street/Hotel St George Station. Remember the wedding scene in "The Godfather"? The setting was the St George roof.

Want To Know More? "AIA Guide to New York City (Brooklyn Heights)," Norval White & Elliot Willensky (2000). For the scandal that surrounded Minister Henry Ward Beecher, read "Other Powers: The Age of Spiritualism, Suffrage, and The Notorious Victoria Woodhull," Barbara Goldsmith (1998). An historical novel is "A House of Her Own," Marcia Rose (1991); "Old Brooklyn Heights: New York's First Suburb," Clay Lancaster (1978) is nonfiction. Visit the landmark Long Island Historical Society at128 Pierrepont St. (-718-222-4111). For an exciting historical account of the Labor Movement in New York, visit the recently reopened Transit Museum (Boerum Place; 1-718-694-5100). Tour restored Borough Hall with Jane Wolff (1-718-855-7882).

WALKING MAP

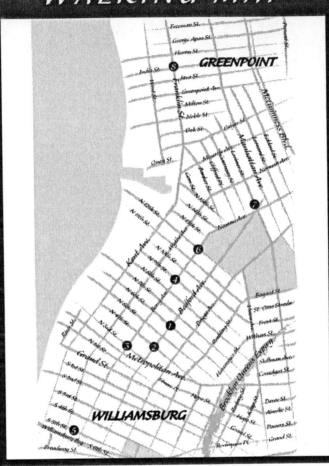

① Bedford Ave. Station   ⑤ Williamsburg Bridge Views

② Realform Girdle Factory   ⑥ Russian Orthodox Church

③ one sixty glass   ⑦ Stylowa

④ Oznot's Dish   ⑧ Astral Apartments

Art, Funk and Cultural Diversity in Brooklyn

Walking Williamsburg and Historic Greenpoint

Williamsburg, Brooklyn is a revitalized neighborhood becoming known for its artistic and trendy ambience, but **Greenpoint**, just next door, with its **Polish restaurants** and **historic row houses and churches**, is much less well known. Both neighborhoods together make a great day's walk in Brooklyn, just across the East River on an easy subway ride, and there's a wide choice of **trendy** or **ethnic restaurants** for lunch.

As early as the 17th century, **Williamsburg** was already a culturally diverse area inhabited by Dutch, French, and Scandanavian farmers and African slaves. By 1800, an enterprising speculator started a ferry to Manhattan, hoping to create a town for those working across the river. Named after the surveyor, Jonathan Williams, the plan failed, but in 1827, thanks to the steam ferry and road building, the Village of Williamsburgh soon became a thriving industrial city. When it was incorporated with Brooklyn, in 1855, the final "h" was dropped from its name. Williamsburg soon became a fashionable suburb for German, Austrian, and Irish industrialists, with hotels, beer gardens, and exclusive clubs. Along the waterfront were docks, shipyards, factories, distilleries, taverns, mills and foundries, including some of the largest industrial firms such as Pfizer, Standard Oil, and Corning Glass, as well as the world's largest sugar refinery. We'll see some vestiges of this history on today's walk.

After the Williamsburg Bridge opened in 1903, thousands of poor and working-class Jews from Eastern Europe moved to the neighborhood from the Lower East Side. Later, Lithuanian, Polish, Russian Orthodox, and Italian enclaves also developed; the latter is the site of annual *festa* in July, called the dancing of the *giglio* (see Special Events). Like other parts of Brooklyn, Williamsburg had its ups and downs over the 20th century. In the 1930s many businesses left and the Hasidic Jewish community expanded to the south. (Hasidic Williamsburg is too far from the main sites on our walk today, but can be left for another day. It is most interesting on Friday nights and Saturday mornings—dress modestly). By 1990 the population was almost half Latino.

In its most recent incarnation, **Williamsburg**, north of the Williamsburg Bridge, has become filled with **artists' residences and studios, art galleries, boutiques and restaurants.** This area, where our walk begins, is easily reached by the **L train** to Bedford Avenue. Begin the **walk** by crossing the street and turning left to see the old **Realform Girdle Company** building (on Bedford between 4–5th Sts.), a small mall of funky shops centered around an antique cast iron stove. Continue in the same direction down Bedford, make a right on **Grand St.** (not to be confused with Grand St. in Manhattan), and walk the few blocks to the River, where there is a **smokestack with a plaque** from the Pfizer company and **beautiful views of the Williamsburg Bridge.** Continue north (right) along the River and turn right on N. 3rd to Berry St. where you can visit **one sixty glass,** a glass blowing artists atelier (160 Berry St.).

Hungry? Continue walking on Berry to 9th St., and you'll reach **Oznot's Dish** (79 Berry/N. 9th St.; 1-718-599-6596, daily 11–4, 6–11, Weekend brunch 10–4, dinner 6–11) with its unusual flea market ambience and Mediterranean food. Or, you may want to save lunch for the Polish restaurants along Manhattan Avenue in Greenpoint, about ½ hour walk away (though officially Greenpoint begins at N. 7th St., unofficially its heart begins on Manhattan Ave.).

According to tradition, **Greenpoint,** a site of little known **architectural treasures,** is where "Brooklynese" dialect originated, as in "Greenpernt." Like Williamsburg, Greenpoint was incorporated into the city of Brooklyn in 1855. It also has a culturally diverse immigration history, though today Polish culture predominates. You can continue walking on Bedford or Berry, and you'll come to the intersection of N. 12th St. and Berry, site of the **Russian Orthodox Church of the Transfiguration** (228 N. 12th St.), dominated by onion-shaped cupolas. Inside is a magnificent central cupola. As you leave the church, continue on Bedford, through McCarren Park to Manhattan Ave. and turn left. This is the heart and main commercial district of the Polish community. Continue the walk and you'll soon come to **Stylowa** (694 Manhattan Avenue; 1-718-383-8993; open daily noon-9) an authentic Polish restaurant with delicious food at rock bottom prices. There are also other Polish restaurants, bakeries, and shops all along Manhattan Avenue.

Greenpoint was transformed from an agricultural area to an industrial center by the mid-18th century, and became known for the five "black arts"—printing, pottery, petroleum and gas refining, glassmaking, and ironmaking, as well as warehousing (along Kent Avenue) and shipbuilding (along the East River). By the end of World War II, all these industries declined, and the character of Greenpoint changed to that of a multiethnic, though largely Polish, community whose residents mostly work elsewhere.

Continue walking along Manhattan Avenue and turn left at Noble St., to reach the beautifully preserved row houses of 19th century Greenpoint on **Milton, Noble, India** and **Java Sts. Milton St.,** between Franklin and Manhattan Ave. has the finest architecture in Greenpoint, crowned by St. Anthony's Church, one of Greenpoint's many historic churches. On **Franklin St.** (184 Franklin, between India and Java, on the east side of the street), the Astral Oil Company (later merged with Standard

Oil), built the **Astral Apartments** for its workers alongside the row houses. Here you have just about reached the East River. You can amble back the way you came, or take the B61 bus back along Manhattan Avenue to the subway.

Directions L train to Bedford Ave.

Want to Know More? The Williamsburg Art Center, 1-718-486-7372 for information on community events. "The first hundred years: 1851–1951: an account of the founding and growth of the Williamsburgh Savings Bank, together with a brief history of the communities served by this bank through its first hundred years" (1951); "The Neighborhoods of Brooklyn," John B. Manbeck, ed. (Neighborhoods of New York Series; 1998).

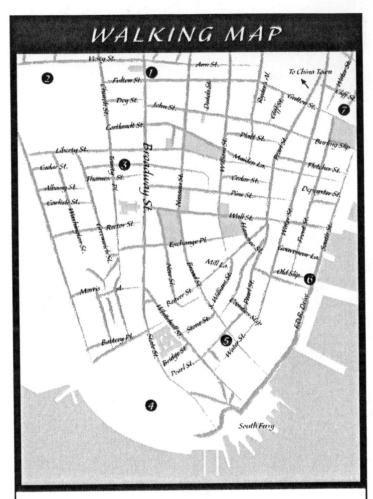

WALKING MAP

Vesey St. • Ann St. • To China Town • Fulton St. • Church St. • Dey St. • John St. • Dutch St. • Ryders Al. • Cliff St. • Gold St. • Jeff St. • Cortlandt St. • Broadway St. • Pearl St. • Burling Slip • Liberty St. • William St. • Maiden Ln. • Fletcher St. • Cedar St. • Thames St. • Cedar St. • Depeyster St. • Albany St. • Nassau St. • Pine St. • Carlisle St. • Rector St. • Wall St. • Exchange Pl. • Greenwich Ln. • Mill Ln. • Old Slip • Morris St. • Beaver St. • William St. • F.D.R. Drive • Battery Pl. • Stone St. • Slip • Water St. • Bridge St. • Pearl St. • State St. • South Ferry

● St. Paul's Chapel   ● Fraunces Tavern

● Ground Zero   ● Vietnam Veterans Memorial

● Trinity Church   ● South Street Seaport

● Battery Park Memorials

Memory and Memorials in Lower Manhattan

Ground Zero, Battery Park's National Monuments, Two Small Museums and the South Street Seaport

This 2-mile walk inspires reflection on our city's central role in the foundation of our nation and its continued pre-eminence as a symbol of America's unity. **Ground Zero**, together with **St. Paul's Chapel's "people's memorials"** to 9–11 commemorate the tragic events that brought together our nation's greatest city with the nation as a whole. The colonial gravesites of **Trinity Church** conjure up the actual inhabitants of this oldest part of the city. Colonial and contemporary heroes of our country are celebrated in the stirring **Battery Park monuments** and **Vietnam Veterans Memorial**, all within a few blocks of each other. The archaeology of the city is revealed in the tiny, fascinating **New York Unearthed Museum**, while in **Fraunces Tavern Museum** you can raise a toast to the Sons of Liberty who shaped our Revolution and gain a new perspective on George Washington (see Special Events, April).

This largely outdoor excursion begins at **Ground Zero** (exit Fulton St./Bway-Nassau station at NW Fulton St.). The first aspect of the Ground Zero area to meet your eye is **St. Paul's Chapel** (Bway at Fulton St.), where George Washington worshipped after his inaugural. Within the Chapel are personal tributes to the victims of 9–11 from all over the world. One block west on Fulton St. to Church St. brings you to the actual **site of**

21

the **World Trade Center**, where enlarged photographs and text inform you about the buildings and the 9–11 attack. As you walk south along the site, the twisted metal **Cross** found in the debris becomes visible. A right turn at Liberty St. provides an overall view of the ongoing site work. Ahead is the **Skywalk** to the beautifully restored **Winter Garden**, the glass-enclosed centerpiece of the World Financial Center, where lunch and free cultural performances can once again be enjoyed (1-212-945-0505); www.worldfinancialcenter.com.

Back on Broadway is **Trinity Church**, originally built in 1697 for Church of England colonists who had "for want of a Temple for worship [felt like citizens of a] conquered Foreign Province...rather than an English Colony." The path to the right of this mid-1800s Gothic Revival building leads to the pre-Revolutionary graveyard; don't miss the text on the first tall gravestone on your left.

Hungry Now Or Later? Between Trinity Church and the next stop, Battery Park are numerous eateries for local office workers sprinkled along Broadway, including a MacDonalds with live piano music (317 Bway; music 11-2). More formal is **Michaels of Broadway** (65 Bway). Battery Park itself contains attractive cafes or you can sit on a bench overlooking the harbour for a BYO lunch. For a major meal in an historical setting, hold out for the **Fraunces Tavern Restaurant** (Pearl and Broad Sts.), a few blocks north of the park. Still further north but within walking distance are the food courts and restaurants of the **South Street Seaport.**

Continuing south on Broadway from Trinity Churchyard, just before Broadway ends is the great **bronze bull**, which appeared mysteriously on Wall St. one day in 1989 and was subsequently moved here (you may want to pat its nose for a Wall St. boom!) **Battery Park**, directly ahead, is more than just a pleasant green space: it is notable for its monuments dedicated to America's highest ideals. First, on the Park corner opposite the American Indian Museum, is a carved plinth celebrating the "ancient and unbroken friendship" (shortlived, as it turned out) between the New Amsterdam Dutch settlers and the Native Americans. Ahead, to the left, is the **Hope Garden**, a flowering alley that now (perhaps temporarily) holds the damaged sphere of the WTC Plaza and an eternal flame to the 9–11 victims. At the Garden's end is a stunning bronze group of immigrants representing those who entered America from Ellis Island through Castle Clinton, the round brick structure just ahead. A path on the right takes you around to the next pair of memorials: a startlingly apt silhouette statue to the "invisible" **Korean War Veterans,** and, as you keep circling, on the river to your right, the new, deeply moving memorial to the **Merchant Mariners,** depicting a rescue at sea. Then, past a small memorial stone to our Norwegian maritime allies in WWII is the **colossal bronze Eagle,** Art Deco in design although only sculpted in 1961, which pays tribute to the seamen of WWII. A recent addition of marble columns with the names of those lost at sea makes a magnificent frame for our Statue of Liberty and Ellis Island in the distance. Then, after a bust of Verrazano—erected with the voluntary donations of Italian Americans—there is a tribute on a plinth to a now largely forgotten group of American combatants, the Wireless Operators lost at sea in WWI, that "war to end all wars."

Exit the Park at this point and cross over to 17 State St. (its entrance occupied by Louise Bourgeoise's fantastical giant spider); around the corner in the courtyard is the fascinating **NY Unearthed Museum** (207 Front St.; 1-212-748-8628; M-F 12–5; free), offering time travel through layers of the city's history. Retrace your steps 1 block north to Pearl St. and walk the few blocks on Pearl to Broad St. for the Fraunces Tavern Museum.

The **Fraunces Tavern Museum** (54 Pearl at Broad St.; 1-212-425-1778; T-Sat 10/11–5; Th until 7; $2–3; Flag Day celebration June 14) introduces you to a setting as old as the founding of our nation. Here, on Dec. 4, 1783, at a "turrtle" dinner in this popular tavern's "Long Room," George Washington bade farewell to his Continental Army commanders, who had recaptured the city after 7 years of British occupation. Washington's toast to his brave fellow-soldiers and other memorabilia related to this generous-hearted patriot is truly inspirational and will enrich your understanding of "the father of our country."

Across the street from the Tavern, at the **Broad Street Lovelace Tavern Dig**, glass panels in the sidewalk (85 Broad St., 1 block off Pearl, around the corner from the building's entrance) display 17th-18th century artifacts revealed by an archaeological dig in this urbane and convivial neighborhood that once housed over a thousand places to dine and hoist a few. Walk the block back to Pearl St. and a few blocks north to Old Slip, where the **Vietnam Veterans Plaza** offers a place to rest and reflect. Its glass wall inscribed with excerpts from letters written by and to those serving in Vietnam forms a moving tribute to the veterans of that controversial conflict. If you want to end your Day here, return to the Bowling Green subway. But if you want to keep going, wend your way north on Front or Water Sts. for about a dozen more blocks until you reach the **South Street Seaport**, a museum, dining and performance complex whose seafaring history is evident in the cobbled streets, riverfront view, and historic brick buildings nearby. Stalwart walkers (actually, it's not more than another ½ mile north and you could hop the uptown Water St. bus) can keep on to **Chinatown** where two additional memorials may be noted. One is the tiny enclosed triangle of **First Shearith Israel Graveyard** (55 St. James Place) in which Sephardic Jewish emigrants from Brazil in the mid-1600s lie buried. Then, at the Chatham Square crossing island into Chinatown proper, is the **Kim Lau Memorial**, an archway with a statue of Confucius, dedicated to the memory of the many Chinese Americans who died in WWII.

Directions Ground Zero is accessed by the #4/5, A/C or #1/2 trains to Fulton St./Bway-Nassau station, the N/R train to City Hall station, or the M6 Broadway bus downtown to Fulton St. To return by subway from the sites between Battery Park and the Vietnam Veterans Memorial, the closest subway is the #4/5 at Bowling Green (opposite the Museum of the American Indian). South St. Seaport's closest subway is the Fulton St./Bway-Nassau station. The beautifully restored PATH/subway station is now open.

Want To Know More? "Unearthing Gotham: The Archeology of New York City," Anne-Marie Cantwell and Diana diZerega Wall (2000). Recent books on the WTC/Ground Zero include

"Twin Towers: The Life of New York City's World Trade Center," Angus Kress Gillespie (2002); "September 11, 2001: A Record of Tragedy, Heroism and Hope," editors of New York Magazine (2002); "NEW YORK SEPTEMBER 11," Magnum Photographers (2002); "After the World Trade Center: Rethinking New York City," eds. Michael Sorkin and Sharon Zukin (2002). Fraunces Tavern Museum Gift Shop offers a selection of books on colonial New York. Several fascinating, colonial-era *policiers* by Maan (also Martin) Meyers (1992–1996) are set within the area of this Day.

WALKING MAP

North Cove

ELYSIAN PARK

STEVENS COLLEGE

❺

NORTH COVE YACHT HARBOR

10TH

HUDSON RIVER

Battery Park City

SOUTH END AV

ALBANY ST

WASHINGTON ST

River St.

RECTOR PLACE

❹

THIRD PLACE

SECOND PLACE

FIRST PLACE

BATTERY PLACE

Bowling Green

BATTERY PLACE

STATE STREET

Pier A

❷

❶

GREENWICH ST

Hoboken, NJ

Manhattan, NY

---

❶ *National Museum of the American Indian*

❷ *Hudson River Esplanade Walk Begins*

❺ *Ferry Terminal to Hoboken*

❹ *Ferry Dock & Landmark Railroad Terminal*

Harbor Perspectives

The National Museum of the American Indian and Heavenly Hoboken

A morning visit to the stellar collections of the **National Museum of the American Indian,** housed in the gorgeous Alexander Hamilton Customs House across from Battery Park begins the day. Then several splendid perspectives of **New York's harbor** illuminate Lower Manhattan's relationship with **Hoboken,** our beautifully preserved neighbor across the Hudson. A delightful stroll up the **Hudson River Esplanade,** a short ferry crossing with a glorious 360-degree view of both shores, and the sweep of Manhattan's skyline from atop a Hoboken hillside are among today's rewards. **Frank Sinatra fans** (and everyone else too) can enjoy a cannoli at Sinatra's favorite Hoboken bakery or dine at a virtual Frank Sinatra Hall of Fame, while **Marlon Brando fans** can stand on the shipping docks made famous in the film classic "On the Waterfront."

Exit the #5 train at the Bowling Green station. There, the grand edifice of the **Smithsonian's National Museum of the American Indian** (1-212-514-3700; daily 10–5, Th 10–8; free) reflects the building's original function as the collection point for New York's customs fees. The heads of the eight "races" of humanity adorn the window arches; twelve statues above the cornice symbolize the world's great trading nations; heroic limestone sculptures portray the four corners of the earth. Inside, the Lobby's walls display Reginald Marsh murals of the city's port.

The Museum's permanent exhibit, "All Roads Are Good," represents Native American perspectives on their heritage.

For the **Hoboken Ferry**, exit the Museum, turn left (west) to the river's edge, then right (north) at the **Hudson River Esplanade** for a 20 minute walk past Battery Park City until you reach Gateway Plaza. Follow the path around the Yacht Harbour to the **NY Waterway Ferry Terminal** (1-800-533-3779; Hoboken ferry every 10–15 minutes weekdays, every ½ hour weekends; $3; bikes permitted). Once docked, access Hoboken's center by leaving the ferry slip (the landmark 1907 **Erie-Lackawanna Railroad Terminal**, with its copper roofing, terrazzo floors and Tiffany glass ceiling is behind you) and proceeding down River St. for 2 blocks. Turn left onto Newark St., where you'll note the century-old **Clam Broth House** (#38; daily, noon-10PM), which still serves its free hot clam broth in the old seaman's barroom. Continue 2 blocks further on to **Washington Street,** Hoboken's main stem.

By the mid-1600s Hoboken had America's first brewery, and by the mid-19th century New Yorkers were rowing across the Hudson to the Elysian Fields, site of America's first challenge baseball game between the Knickerbockers and the New Yorkers in 1864. Hoboken's German beer gardens and raucous Oktoberfest were also a big hit with New Yorkers. By the late 1800s, Hoboken was a major shipping, railroad, and factory town—the folks in Greenwich Village could smell the Maxwell House coffee plant's redolent odors—and there were expanding employment opportunities for working men of all ethnic backgrounds. The dockworkers, particularly Italians, shaped Hoboken's "tough guy" image (many of its dockworkers played in Brando's film) and brought relative prosperity to the area until the 1930s Depression killed off much of its industry and related rail and shipping networks.

Washington Street has the atmosphere of a typical American small town in the golden age from the turn of the century through the 1920s. **Carlo's Italian City Hall Bakery** (95

Washington), where Frank Sinatra's father, Hoboken's Fire Chief, and his famous son, were frequent customers, is only one of many traditional (and newer) restaurants on the street. Stroll at leisure past Washington's ecclectic mix of residential and commercial architectural styles (a 6 block detour at 8th St. to 841 Grand St. takes you to Frank Sinatra's boyhood home).

Hungry? There's no shortage of choices for lunch. Sinatra fanatics can turn left on Washington at 2nd St. to Grand St. for **Leo's Grandvous Restaurant** (200 Grand St; 1-201-659-9467; lunch 11:30–2 weekdays only; dinner 5–11 weekdays, 4–9:30 Sun). This neighborhood fixture is devoted to Frank Sinatra. Further down, near the Elysian Fields at Washington and 11th St., there's a trace of Hoboken's German immigration in **Helmer's German Restaurant** (1036 Washington; 1-201-963-3333; M-Th noon-10; F/Sat 8-11).

For the **Stevens College Overlook**, turn up the slight hill at the corner of Washington and 10th St. to the college's main walkway; the Gatehouse faces a grey rock outcropping noted in Henry Hudson's 1609 log of the Half Moon. The Wesley Lowe Center, on a bluff above the Hudson, offers benches and picnic tables with unparalleled views of Manhattan skylines from the George Washington Bridge to the Battery. Identifiable from right to left are Battery Park City; the Woolworth Building's spire and the columned pinnacle of the Con Ed building on 14th St. Foregrounded on the river are the Chelsea Piers athletic buildings; the gold pinnacle of the Met Life Building; the Empire State at 34th St. and the glittering scalloped spire of the Chrysler Building. Movie helicopters often circle around to obtain aerial views of New York for film productions.

Still Hungry? Try the early-bird dinner at **Amanda's** (908 Washington St./10th St. [down the hill from Stevens College]; 1-201-798-0101; reservations recommended, especially Sat).

To return home, continue to the ferry or PATH train station by descending from the Stevens campus to lovely Hudson St., which boasts a charming mix of brownstones with carved decorative columns and cornices, fieldstones with scalloped mansard roofs and wrought iron railings, and 19th century brick homes with tight "butter" joints. Also on Hudson St., the **Hoboken Historical Museum** (#1301; 1-201-656-2240; T-W-Th 5–9; Sat-Sun, noon-5) is worth a visit.

Directions To the National Museum of the American Indian, the #5 train to Bowling Green station, the N/R to Whitehall Street or the Broadway bus M1 or M6 downtown to Bowling Green. If you return by PATH to Manhattan, you'll need 6 quarters for each one way fare. Hoboken's PATH entrance is adjacent to the Waterways Ferry Terminal at which you arrived. PATH permits bikes weekends and non-rush hour weekdays (8:30–3:30 and after 6:30 PM).

Want To Know More? Museum of the American Indian website: www.AmericanIndian.si.edu. The essay collection, "Yuppies Invade My House at Dinnertime: A Tale of Brunch, Bombs and Gentrification in an American City," Joseph Barry and John Derevlany, eds. (1987) contains photographs of the city. Randy Tarabarrelli's "Sinatra: Beyond The Legend" (1997) includes the local color of the singer's years in Hoboken. Nathaniel Hawthorne's "House of the Seven Gables" contains a beautifully detailed description of the ferry ride to Hoboken.

WALKING MAP

9th Ave.
W 23rd St
W 27th St
W 26th St
W 25th St
W 24th St
W 29th St
W 29th St
5th Ave.
Madison Ave.

7th Ave.
Greenwich Ave.
W 22nd St
W 21st St
W 20th St
W 19th St
W 18th St
W 17th St
W 16th St
W 15th St
W 14th St
W 13th St
W 12th St
W 11th St
W 10th St
W 9th St
W 8th St
Waverly Pl.

Park Ave. S.
E 24th St
E 23rd St
E 21th St
E 20th St
E 19th St
E 18th St
E 17th St

Irving Pl.
Broadway
4th Ave.
3rd Ave.

Jones St.
Cornelia St.
Bleecker St.
Sullivan St.
Thompson St.
W. Houston St.
Mercer St.
Bond St.
Lafayette St.

E 8th St
E 3rd St
E 4th St
E 6th St
E 7th St
St Marks Pl.
E 9th St
E 10th St
E 12th St
E 13th St

---

1. *Triangle Fire Site*
2. *Washington Square Arch*
3. *Forbes Magazine Galleries*
4. *New School*
5. *Parson's Gallery*
6. *Salamagundi*
7. *Theodore Roosevelt Birthplace*
8. *Gramercy Park*
9. *Block Beautiful*
10. *Cooper Union*
11. *Russian Turkish Bath*

Democrats and Plutocrats

Lower Fifth Avenue and Union Square to Ladies Mile and Gramercy Park

Today's moderate length, all-seasons city walk links historic and contemporary sites woven into New York's rich, colorful, and durable social fabric. The excursion begins in **Greenwich Village at the site of the 1911 Triangle Shirtwaist Factory fire**, a tragedy for poor immigrants that evoked universal outrage and was a catalyst for labor reform. The route proceeds up **lower Fifth Avenue** with stops for spirit-lifting art: fanciful, exquisite *objets* in the family collections of the **Forbes Magazine Galleries**; American art in the **Salamagundi Club**; provocative political art in the **New School for Social Research**. Rallies and protests are a proud New York tradition at the next destination, **Union Square Park**. Within a decade of the Triangle Fire, working men and women demonstrated here for a living wage and decent working conditions. Close by, in the fine shops of **Ladies Mile**, their privileged counterparts, the "carriage trade" purchased gowns and jewels appropriate for the elegant life-style of **Gramercy Square**. **ABC Carpets**, a gorgeous oriental bazaar purported to be our "**most beautiful store**" offers opportunities for lunch, browsing, and shopping. The route continues to nearby **Theodore Roosevelt Birthplace**, a precisely replicated Victorian brownstone and then proceeds to **Gramercy Square**, known as "**the most beautiful city square**." A walk along the official "**most beautiful city block**" follows. The excursion concludes at the galleries of **Cooper Union**, the city's only free university, established in 1859 by industrialist Peter Cooper specifically to provide education for the working class. Admission is still based solely on scholarship and potential for creative excellence. Architect David Liebeskind, designer of the complex to be built at the World Trade Center is a Cooper Union graduate.

To begin this walk, take the N/R subway to the 8th St. station for the **site of the Triangle Shirtwaist Factory fire** at 23 Washington Place (walk along Waverly Pl. to Greene St; turn on Green; walk 1 block to Washington Pl.). Here on Saturday, March 25, 1911, 146 sewing machine girls between the ages of 13 and 23 died needlessly, trapped by locked doors and inadequate fire exits. Many jumped to their deaths, their hair and enveloping clothing in flames. A child looking up from the street exclaimed, "The birds are on fire." The **plaque** that marks the site isn't impressive; nor was the compensation paid—$75.00 to the families of 23 victims. But the event led to the passage of safety laws and eventually the founding of the International Ladies Garment Workers Union.

Continue east to **Washington Square Arch.** Originally a wooden structure erected in 1889 to celebrate the centennial of George Washington's inaugural, the Arch marks the beginning of Fifth Avenue. Walk north along the avenue's west side. A short diversion on 11th St. takes you to #18 where in 1970, an 1845 Greek Revival townhouse was unintentionally blown up by a student group making bombs in the basement. (A lesson for the new millennium: the house could never be put together again.) Return to 5th Ave. for the **Forbes Magazine Galleries** (62 5th Ave./12th St.;1-212-206-5548; T/W/F/Sat 10-4; free) The extensive holdings are unquestionably unique: exquisite Faberge Imperial Easter Eggs, armadas of model boats, battalions of toy soldiers "on parade," presidents' private letters, and monopoly sets that illustrate the evolution and diffusion of the game. Background music (stirring not loud) and minimal automation add to the charm of this small museum.

The **New School for Social Research** (66 W. 12th St. between 5th/6th Aves.) was the "university in exile" for faculty escaping Nazi Germany during the 1930s; the 12th St. building has art on many floors. Take the elevator to the 7th to see the **Jose Clemente Orozco Mural Room** and the etching "Where Is My Daughter?", a poignant indictment of the barbarous Pinochet regime in Chile. Return to 5th Ave. and continue north, passing pleasant 19th century residences. Student art, including superb fashion design, is often on view at **Parson's Gallery** (5th Ave./13th St.). Cross the Avenue to **Salamagundi**, America's first artists' club (#47;1-212-255-7740; daily 1-5; free), housed in a vintage 1853 landmark building. Membership has included John Singer Seargeant, Childe Hassan, and Charles Dana Gibson, whose mass market image, the Gibson Girl, wore a shirtwaist as an emblem of freedom from conformity and cosseting as well as corset and bustle. See the perfectly preserved parlor and the stairwell leading up to a skylight. Then continue north again on 5th Ave. and turn east on 17th St. to #16, **Beads of Paradise**, a colorful shop with hand crafted jewelry from all parts of the world.

Hungry Now or Later? Next door, **Havana Central** (18 E.17th St.) has ample Cuban sandwiches. **Chopt** (#20) offers fresh customized salads. **Union Square Park**, our next destination, has a popular **Farmers' Market** (W, F, Sat are the best days.) Shop here and lunch on a park bench or enjoy the **Park's outdoor café**. On Broadway, **in ABC Carpets** (#881-887) **Le Pain Quotidien** is a communal dining experience; also **in ABC** is pretty **Pipa tapas y mas** with a good Spanish menu. Fresh food at **Friend of a Farmer** (77 Irving Pl.; 1-212-477-2188.) draws crowds. Directly across the street is a well-priced lunch in the 170 year-old landmark **Pete's Tavern** (129 E.18th St). O'Henry may have written "Gift of the Magi" here. Further downtown, **Danal** (90 E.10th at Lexington) has cats (not to eat), antiques, and good country cooking.

Enter **Union Square Park** at 17th St. The largest mass meeting ever held here was in 1927 to protest the execution of anarchists Sacco and Vanzetti, who were falsely accused of murder. Recently the entire park became a candle-lit, flower strewn community shrine to those who died in the World Trade Center on 9–11. Some mementoes remain in the 14th St. subway station. The park's statues are particularly fine: See **Mahatma Gandhi**, a new favorite, at the southwest corner. Exit the park on the northern border near the statue of **Marquis de Lafayette** by Bartholdi, sculptor of the Statue of Liberty. Then continue north on Broadway. Along this eastern section of **Ladies Mile** many of the establishments that once catered to the families of the robber barons have retained their magnificence. See the elegant "Prague Renaissance" façade of the former Lord and Taylor at 901 Broadway/20th St.

Walk east on 20th St. to the **Theodore Roosevelt Birthplace** (20 E. 20th; 1-212-260-1616; W-Sun 9–5; closed M-T; tours on the hour until 4; $3) This replicated building has the decorative and structural features of the house TR knew as a boy, including the outdoor gymnasium built to help him overcome childhood asthma. These Roosevelts were undoubtedly well-received at homes on adjacent **Gramercy Park Square** (1831). The city's only remaining private park, it is generally open to the public the first Saturday in May. See the **grand establishments** along the southern edge: the 1845 **Players Clubhouse** (#16), founded by actor Edwin Booth, whose statue is in the center of the park and the 1884 **National Arts Club** (#15; 1-212-475-3424), which was the residence of Governor Samuel Tilden. The 1859 **Brotherhood Synagogue** (#23) was a **Friends Meeting House** and retains the austere Quaker style. John Barrymore lived in the 1890 **Hamilton Fish House** (#19). Turn south here and then enter **Block Beautiful** (19th St. between 3 rd Ave. and Irving Place). The very pretty and seemingly delicate row of pastel stuccoed buildings attracted a bohemian circle in the 1920s and '30s. Actress Ethel Barrymore commented on the party scene: "I went there [to #151] in the evening a young girl and came away in the morning an old woman."

The route continues south on Irving Place and down 4th Ave. to **Cooper Union Galleries** (E. 7th St./Astor Place; 1-212-353-4100; M-F 11–7; cl. Sun) which exhibit the work of the renowned faculty, students, and prominent figures in the contemporary art world. Abraham Lincoln is among the fiery radicals who have spoken in the **Lecture Hall**. His 1860 anti-slavery "right makes might"speech won him the presidential nomination.

Before heading home, **Cloisters Café** (238 E 9th/3rd Ave.) offers stained glass windows and a pretty garden for a relaxing coffee. For a blissfully restful conclusion to this beautiful day, we recommend the **Russian and Turkish Baths** (268 E.10th St./1st Ave.; 1-212-473-8806; $22 for sauna, steam and towels, and a platza treatment, which makes you "rosy" for $30.00).

Directions Begin/return from the #N/R stop at 8th Street Station or the #6 stop at Astor Place.

Want To Know More? See "'Republic of Dreams' Greenwich Village: The American Bohemia, 1910–1960," Ross Wetzsteon (2002); novels "Union Square," Meredith Tax (2001) and "The Alienist," Caleb Carr (1995); and Leon Stein's history, "Triangle Fire" (2001). Visit The Bread and Roses Cultural Project at Union 1199 Headquarters, 310 W43 St.

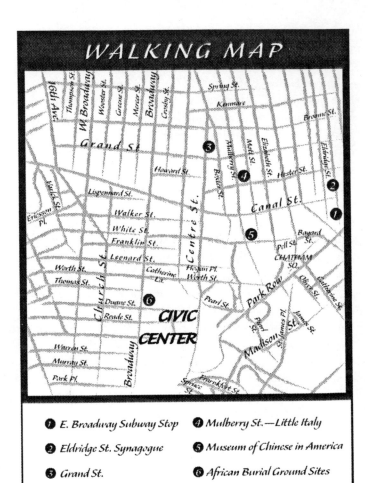

WALKING MAP

- **1** E. Broadway Subway Stop
- **2** Eldridge St. Synagogue
- **3** Grand St.
- **4** Mulberry St. — Little Italy
- **5** Museum of Chinese in America
- **6** African Burial Ground Sites

Strangers to our Shores

The Eldridge Street Synagogue, Little Italy, Chinatown and "Little Africa"

Today's mile or so walk—choose a **Tuesday or Thursday** for access to all the sites—illuminates the deep ethnic roots of "strangers to our shores," and the transitions in our immigrant neighborhoods. The excursion begins with the ornate, century-old **Eldridge Street Synagogue** on the once-Jewish Lower East Side. It then proceeds to **Little Italy's Mulberry Street**, where a recent *risorgiemento* has expanded restaurant and cafe life. In adjacent **Chinatown**, now a magnet for many Asian groups beyond its original Cantonese settlers, the little-known but highly informative **Museum of the Chinese in America** educates the visitor about the social and economic life of this vibrant area. A short walk away is the **African American Burial Ground complex**, an artistic commemoration of the historic area called "Little Africa" during the colonial period. **Ethnic lunch** and **shopping** adds to the day.

The F train East Broadway station is only 3 blocks east of Eldridge St. There, set like a gem among the tenements that once housed eastern European Jews, is the flamboyant facade of the **Eldridge Street Synagogue** (12 Eldridge, between Forsyth and Canal Sts.; 1-212-219-0888; 1 hour tours T and Th 11:30 and 2:30; Sun, hourly from 11-3 but call to confirm; $3–5). Be there for the **11:30 tour.** Knowledgeable guides recreate the vanished world of the synagogue and its congregation. The Synagogue (1887), unlike many others nearby, was not originally a church, but was built specifically to Jewish design and purpose by its well-to-do orthodox congregation. Before WWI, over 800 members walked from their workplaces or homes to its Sabbath services. With changing demographics, the synagogue fell into disuse and disrepair, but is now undergoing renovation. Though not yet completed, it attracts several dozen people for Friday night and Saturday morning services, and is frequently used for weddings and other events.

From the Synagogue, **Little Italy** is reached by a short stroll north to Grand Street and 4 blocks west across the Bowery. While Grand St.'s once-thronged Jewish dry goods emporiums and Italian bridal shops have transmogrified into Chinese markets, and the imposing Bowery banks are now rental shops for Chinese wedding outfits, **Grand Street** west of the Bowery retains its Italian flavor. Notable on Grand St. are the Italian cheese and pasta shops **Di Paolo** (#206), **Alleva** (#188) and **Piemonte Ravioli** (#190), where a wonderful array of Italian specialities are available at less than uptown prices. On **Mulberry Street**, a left turn takes you to the heart of Little Italy, with scores of dining establishments for every taste and pocketbook.

In the 19th century Italian immigrants were northerners who settled around Greenwich Village. From the late 1870s on, Calabrians, Neapolitans, Sicilians and other southern Italians settled today's Little Italy, mythologized in classics such as "The Godfather" and "Moonstruck." The clubhouses where the old men played cards and conducted "business" all day are mostly gone, along with the markets selling rabbits, sheep heads and top grade steaks and chops, but the Church of the Most Precious Blood still hosts the annual Feast of San Gennaro (see Special Events, September) and several of the street's traditional, unpretentious restaurants remain.

Hungry? Lunchtime on **Mulberry and the nearby streets** offers numerous *prix fixe* specials. Some old favorites are **Luna's** (112 Mulberry), which has served a neighborhood clientele for decades and **Puglia** (187 Hester), a once raffish eatery whose menu offered half a sheep's head with eyeball for $1.00 and boasted a singing waitress; it is now gussied up for tourists. **Cha Cha's** (111 Mulberry) has a lovely garden; **La Bella Ferrara** (126 Mulberry) has delicious, inexpensive Italian pastries to take home or eat along with a cappuccino.

The afternoon continues on Mulberry St. across Canal Street, the older boundary of **Chinatown**, whose diversity is apparent in its many types of cuisine. As in San Francisco and Boston, the neighboring Italian and Chinese communities of New York, though cheek by jowl, have very few political or economic alliances. The last decades of Chinese entrepreneurial expansion across Canal St. engendered some resentment in the Italian community, and, in fact, spurred the latter's *risorgiemento*. The Chinese, for their part, would like to overcome the greater political clout of Little Italy. But one interesting interaction still exists: the Chinese (formerly Italian) funeral homes on Mulberry St, opposite Columbus Park, continue the custom of driving the deceased around the neighborhood to the strains of an Italian band.

The small but enlightening **Museum of the Chinese in America** (70 Mulberry St. 2nd fl; 1-212-619-4785; T-Sun, noon-5; $1–3), housed in the century-old, once-Italian PS 23, explains much that underlies the Chinatown scene from the past to the present. On the sidewalk by the Museum, Chinese artistry is available on handpainted t-shirts and there are inexpensive, authentic Chinese products at the **dry goods and herbal shops** between 74 and 78 Mulberry St. Alongside Columbus Park you can get your fortune told or have your shoes repaired on the street!

A few blocks south through Chinatown's Columbus Park to Foley Square and Duane St. is the **African Burial Ground** complex in the area once known as "Little Africa." In the 1700s, free and slave Africans comprised about 20% of the city's population, and 5 to 6 acres around Duane St. and Broadway were allocated for African American burials. A 1991 excavation revealed the presence of the long forgotten African Burial Ground. Today, this important aspect of Lower Manhattan's history is expressed through contemporary African American art works. **Foley Square's** soaring sculpture, "The Triumph of the Spirit," a stylized Bamana (Mali) headress representing male and female Chi Wara antelopes, symbolizes the joint human effort for a fruitful harvest. A right turn up Duane St. to Bway leads to a **grassy plot with an historical plaque** marking the burial ground site. The lobby of the **Federal Office Building at 290 Duane** (M-F, 9-5; expect an X-ray check; have photo ID; ask for the Information Desk, where there are excellent brochures and possibly an exhibit educator; no photographs) houses 4 artistic expressions of African American culture. On the floor is the **New Ring Shout**, a dance circle inscribed with texts related to slavery and America's multiculturalism. On the wall to its right is the silk-screened **mural "Renewal,"** a tribute to the Africans and their descendants who, along with others, built colonial New York. Ahead on the left, the heroic sculpture "**Africa Rising**" celebrates our nationhood and common humanity. At the far end of the lobby, high on a wall to the right, a **tile mosaic of skulls and faces** rising to a New York cityscape suggests the urban substratum of the African Burial Ground.

Directions The Eldridge St. Synagogue is reached by F train to the East Bway station and a short walk west to Eldridge St. The 2nd Ave. busses M15 and M22 also run close to the Synagogue. Bus M103 down the Bowery takes you close to all the sites. All subways are near the African Burial Ground for your return: the #4/5 City Hall-Brooklyn Bridge stop; the N/R City Hall station; the A/C on Chambers and Church Sts.; and the #2/3/1/9 on Chambers St. and W. Bway.

Want To Know More? For books about the Lower East Side, see our Grand Street Circle day. For the infamous Five Points area of 19th century Little Italy and Chinatown see "The Gangs of New York," Herbert Asbury (1928, reprinted 2001) along with Martin Scorcese's film of the same name (2003) and "Five

Points: The 19th century New York City Neighborhood that Invented Tap Dance, Stolen Elections and Became the World's Most Notorious Slum," Tyler Anbinder (2001). Little Italy is the setting for the *policier* "A Bone in the Throat," by Anthony Bourdain (1995). Studies of New York's Chinatown are "Tea That Burns: A Family Memoir of Chinatown," Bruce Edward Hall (1998); Amy Li's "Under Western Eyes: Personal Notes from an Asian American" (1987); and Peter Kwong's "The New Chinatown" (1987). Leslie Glass' "Stealing Time" (1999) is a *policier* set in the area. Sherrill D. Wilson's "New York City's African Slaveholders: A Social and Material Culture History" (1994) and M.A. Harris' "A Negro History Tour of Manhattan" (1968) illuminate lower Manhattan's historical "Little Africa."

Truth and Beauty

WALKING MAP

Prospect Park

Osborne Garden

The Brooklyn Museum

Eastern Parkway

Washington Ave

Botanic Garden

Native Flora Garden

Cranford Rose Garden

Cherry Esplanade

Magnolia Plaza Visitor Center Entrance

Flatbush Ave

Rock Garden

Washington Ave

Butterll Bushes

Prospect Park

Children's Garden

① Entrance to BBG	⑥ Rock Garden
② Herb Garden	⑦ Rose Garden
③ Shakespeare Garden	⑧ Osborne Garden
④ Japanese Garden	⑨ Subway 2/3
⑤ Terrace Cafe	⑩ The Brooklyn Museum

World Class

The Brooklyn Museum and the Brooklyn Botanic Garden

The **Brooklyn Museum of Art** and the **Brooklyn Botanic Garden** are vital commuity institutions that enjoy international reputations, attracting folks from as far away as Bombay and as near as Bensonhurst. The **Museum**, the second largest fine arts museum in the United States, exhibits art from all parts of the world and all periods up to and including very trendy modern times. "**The Dinner Party**," sculptor Judy Chicago's pivotal feminist work has become a part of the permanent collection and will be on view beginning in 2004. The museum's brilliance is complemented by the serene beauty and atmosphere of its bucolic neighbor, the **Brooklyn Botanic Garden**, where two restrictions mystify visitors: you may not remove clothing, specifically shoes or shirts, nor may you bring in food. Seem oppressive? Possibly, but it has worked since 1910. And, as we say in Brooklyn, "*If it ain't broke, don't fix it.*"

Take the #2/3 subway to Eastern Parkway/Brooklyn Museum station for the **Brooklyn Museum of Art** (200 Eastern Parkway; 1-718-638-5000; W-Sun10-5; Sat 11-6; suggested admission; free 1st Sat each month to11PM). The **new entrance and facade** is designed by the architectural firm of Stuart Polshek whose projects include the Rose Center (American Museum of Natural History) and the Clinton Library. Each floor is a treasure trove; the **illustrated gallery guide available in**

the lobby will help you to be selective in your viewing. Here are some favorites.

On the **first floor**, imposing Northwest Coast totems, peering over the **Art of the Americas Gallery** evoke school-trip memories for many New Yorkers. Here, too, are the sacred Hopi kachina dolls and **the Americas' oldest extant tapestry, the Paracas Mantle** (Peru, 100 BCE), whose vibrant border pictures of animals, people, flora, and deities gives insight into this pre-Incan culture. The **African Gallery** draws connections between art, royalty, and leadership. Try "reading" the linguist's staff, carried by an *Oba's* (king's) attendant. For example, a cat struggling to get out of a bag symbolizes the political astuteness of staying out of "the king's bag," or affairs of state. An immense beaded headdress from the Cameroons is topped by the mythic bird, *Olakun*, who brings messages to the *Oba* from ancestral spirits and also inspires artists. On the **second floor** in the **Asian Galleries**, among the Chinese works, an image may echo through thousands of years: a wine vessel in the form of a goose (206 BCE), for example, is recreated in the bronzes of several successive dynasties. Japanese lacquer ware and Korean celadon pottery are visual poems.

The **third floor's** Beaux Arts Court, an Edwardian ballroom, is used for performances and receptions. **The Egyptian Collection** is called the best outside of Cairo. Don't overlook **mosaics from ancient synagogues.** Exotic treats on the **fourth floor** are Victorian Fantasy Furniture and—for fashionistas—a fascinating historical shoe display. J.D.Rockefeller's Moorish smoking room (1885) was a landmark for the new profession of interior decorating. **Fifth floor** galleries trace the development of **American painting in innovative displays**—living spaces appointed with furniture and embellishments appropriate to historical periods. Edward Hick's "Peaceable Kingdom"and Eastman Johnson's profound Civil War work "**A Ride for Liberty-Fugitive Slaves**" are not to be missed. You won't be able to miss Albert Bierstadt's ode to the wonders of the American west: the huge, heroic "**A Storm in the Rocky Mountains.**"

Hungry? The museum has a **cafeteria** and, **on weekends, the Mummy Café.** There are benches for BYO in the Schiff Sculpture Garden, which has architectural details from demolished city buildings. Outside the Museum and across the Parkway is **Tom's Luncheonette,** a vintage diner (782 Washington Ave.; closes at 4). For an alfresco lunch, enjoy the **Terrace Café** in the Brooklyn Botanic Garden.

Leave the museum on the lower level; walk diagonally to the left, continuing through the parking lot to the gate of the **Brooklyn Botanic Garden** (1-718-623-7220; Apr-Sept T-F 8-6; weekends/holidays 10-6; cl. M and some holidays; weekend tours at 1; adm. $3; no pets, blankets, jogging, picnicking, or sitting on the lawn [except for the Cherry Esplanade]). **Pick up the map as you enter.** The following route, highlighting some special places, takes you around the garden in a clock-wise direction to the subway.

Inspiration for gardeners begins at the **Herb Garden** with 300 medicinal, culinary, fragrant, and ornamental herbs arranged in a 16th century Elizabethan love knot design. The **Japanese Hill-and-Pond Garden**, ahead on the right was designed by Takeo Shiota in 1914 to be "a garden more beautiful than all others in the world"; the topography suggests Japan's rocky coastline and steep mountains; trees, plants, and structures are patterned to create an impression of deep perspective.

Left, in the English **Shakespeare Garden**, labels refer to the plays. In Spring, when flowers are "abloom," one fully appreciates the imagery affixed to a lily bed: "To gild refined gold, to paint the lily is wasteful and ridiculous excess." Directly ahead is the **Fragrance Garden** with Braille labels. Close your eyes and inhale the perfumes. Which can you identify?

Continue S, then W around the perimeter of the garden. Across the broad lawn is **The Plant Family Collection**, a graceful landscape with blooms that mature and change with the seasons.

Nearby is the Children's Garden Project, where city kids get to plant, tend, and finally reap what they sow. At the corner, is the flamboyant short-lived **Peony Garden** and the **Rock Garden**, whose boulders are dotted with flowers and colorful shade plants. Directly ahead, gorgeous in their special times are **the Cranford Rose Garden** (June-Sept), the **Cherry Esplanade** (Apr-May) and the **Lilac Collection** (late Spring). For **a lovely panoramic view**, climb the stairs to the **Overlook**. On this level, the **Osborne Garden,** an elegant azalea-banked lawn with classic architectural details stretches to Eastern Parkway and the subway. As you stroll towards the gate, you may catch a glimpse of a bride posing for wedding photographs, a sign of good luck here in Brooklyn.

Directions: Take the #2/3 train to Eastern Parkway station for Brooklyn Museum and Brooklyn Botanic Garden (the #4/5 train permits an easy platform change to the #2/3 at Nevins St.).

Want To Know More "Masterpieces in the Brooklyn Museum," Harry N. Abrams (1988); "The Complete Illustrated Guide to Prospect Park and The Brooklyn Botanic Garden," R. Berenson and N. deMause (2001). See website BrooklynMuseumofArt.org/visit/permanentcollection

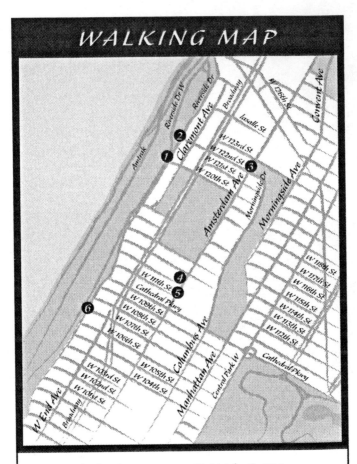

WALKING MAP

1 Riverside Church   **4** St. John the Divine

2 President Grant's Tomb   **5** Children's Sculpture Garden

3 Morningside Heights Overlook   **6** Nicholas Rorich Museum

A Divine Day on Upper Broadway

St. John the Divine, the Nicholas Roerich Museum and President Grant's Tomb

Mix and match the sacred and the secular, the intellectual, the beatific, and the earthy on today's journey along the great avenues of Manhattan's Upper West Side. The first site is decorous **Riverside Church.** At the behest of its patron, John D. Rockefeller, its stone carving and stained glass were the finest available in1926. Across Riverside Drive is the neo-classic **President Grant's Tomb,** a beautiful national monument that memorializes Grant as a peacemaker whose brilliant strategies ended the Civil War, keeping the nation intact and establishing universal emancipation. The route continues to the triumphal **Cathedral Church of St. John the Divine,** where works of art teach the stories of the scriptures, and good works endeavor to alleviate the world's suffering. A stroll back to Broadway includes a lunch break. The final spiritual site today is the very special **Nicholas Roerich Museum,** which exhibits the art and encourages the philosophy of Roerich (1874–1947), the Russian mystic who was at once painter, pacifist, poet, yogi, diplomat, and teacher.

Begin the day with **a ride on Riverside Drive.** Board the M5 bus at 72nd St. and Broadway. The route is N to 120 St., passing grand mansions, monuments, and the fabled huge apartment houses that overlook the Hudson River. Enter **Riverside Church** (490 Riverside Drive; Visitor Center 1-212-870-6700; M-Sat 11-3; Sun 12:30-4; $1). The interior where Martin Luther King gave his historic anti-Vietnam War sermon is quietly restrained while the famous bells of the **Rockefeller Carillion** are engagingly exuberant; they chime and thunder every sixty minutes. **Christ Chapel** is lovely. Take the elevator to the carillon; climb the open stairway past the bells to the windswept outside observation deck that offers a 360 degree views of the city.

Cross the drive at 122nd St. to **President Grant's Tomb** (1-212 666-1640;W-Sun 9-5). A visit here is more than a valuable history lesson. National Park Service guides are pleased to point out decorative features: mosaics, classical friezes and reliefs that demonstrate the Victorian retro infatuation with antiquity.

Walk east (right) on 122nd St. Nearby are two influential modern seminaries: **Jewish Theological** (3080 Broadway) and **Union Theological** (on120th-122nd Sts. between Bway and Claremont Ave.) The former houses a stellar collection of Hebraica; nearby streets and squares honor prominent theologians.

If the pace is slow and the weather fine, continue east to Amsterdam Avenue where young travelers congregate at the **overlook of Morningside Heights** near the **monument to Carl Schurz,** German Jewish immigrant who was a crusading journalist for human rights. Return to Broadway and walk south (downtown) between the **Barnard** and **Columbia University** campuses. Cross the streets near 116th St. through Columbia's classic quad to see Daniel French's splendid statue of **Alma Mater** seated grandly before the great domed and colonnaded **Low Library**. Turn right (south) at Amsterdam Ave.

Enter **the Cathedral Church of St. John the Divine** (112th St.; 1-212-316-7540). In the tradition of Europe's magnificent medieval cathedrals on which building continued in fits and starts for centuries, **St. John's** is still, after a hundred years, a work in progress. Massive as Rome's St. Peters, but unlike its old world antecedents, this modern institution offers cutting edge performances and a progressive social agenda. Radiating chapels celebrate arts and letters and call attention to the plight of oppressed people, of the earth, of endangered animals. New Yorkers bring their pets to St. John's for the remarkable **Blessing of the Animals**, when—accompanied by new age music—llamas and elephants lead other creatures, large and small, in procession to the altar (see Special Events, October). Adjacent, the **Children's Sculpture Garden**, (111th St.) enfolds the biggest, scariest sculptural work in New York, maybe the world. Ceramic plaques contain messages of peace by Ghandi, Thoreau, and John Lennon.

Hungry? Across Amsterdam Ave. between 110th and 111th Sts., the **Hungarian Pastry Shop, V and T Pizza, Columbia Cottage (Chinese), and Miss Mamie's Spoonbread** offer student atmosphere and student eats. Or continue W to **Broadway** for **La Rosita**, Spanish-Cuban (#2409) and **Le Monde**, a bistro (#2885). On the way to **Tom's Restaurant** (Broadway/112th S)—where Seinfeld and his friends crowded the booths for many sit-com seasons—pass **Labyrinth**, the best area bookstore. **Henry's** (Bway/105th St) is a favorite for a moderately priced good lunch, and it's near the next site.

After lunch, walk west on 107 St. to the **Nicholas Rorich Museum.** (319 W. 107th St.; 1-212-864-7752;T-Sun 2-5; free.) The pretty, white town house near Riverside Drive looks particularly gracious and inviting. But, no invitation is required to enter. Roerich's great diplomatic achievement is the "Roerich Pact," which provides for international protection in war and peace of monuments and cultural institutions. His stylized paintings—exotic landscapes of the Himalayas, iconic figures and symbols—have an Art Deco feeling that is at once bold, dramatic, strangely beautiful, and certainly original. Tapestries and solid hand-crafted furniture add even more color and character.

Return to Broadway with the special feeling of having been privy to the interior of one of the city's lovely homes. Energy to spare? Turn right (south) and join the natives proceeding down-town by foot or bus to 80th St., where many make an abrupt stop at **Zabars** (#2255) to pick up dinner or restock with some of the best eats in town.

Directions Take M5 bus from 72nd St and Broadway to 120th St. Or take the #1/9 local to 116th St.-Broadway station and walk to 120th St. Return via #1/9 local at 110th St. station or #2/3 at 95th St station. The nearest subway to Zabars is the #1/9 and #2/3 stop at 72nd St and Broadway.

Want To Know More? Website is roerich.org. See "History of Renaissance Art," Frederick Hart (2002). Two exceptionally good historical novels about cathedrals are Edward Rutherford's "Sarum" (1992) and Ken LaFollette's "Pillars of the Earth" (1996).

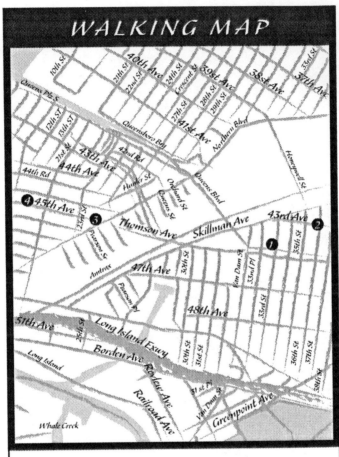

WALKING MAP

1 MoMA Queens   3 P.S.1 at Courthouse Square

2 Museum for African Art   4 45th Ave. Walk 11th-21st Sts.

Queens Modern

MoMA QNS, Museum for African Art and P.S.1 Contemporary Art Center

The pleasure of this day is the opportunity to visit unique museum spaces in Long Island City, **Queens,** where the sites are cool, the crowds are hip and the art is hot. Only the food—the cuisines of the most culturally diverse small community in the world—may be hotter. **MoMA QNS** is a temporary home for Manhattan's **Museum of Modern Art** (until 2005). For MoMA regulars, seeing a favorite work such as Picasso's "Demoiselles d'Avignon," here in a converted Swingline staple factory is akin to a surprise encounter with old friends in dramatic new surroundings. Picasso, captivated by the energy and vivacity of African art, masked the "demoiselles," and modernism was born. Today, after viewing the great painting, see the source of the artist's invention in the **Museum for African Art**, where Africa's awesome aesthetic sensibility is now on view in its many cultural styles. The excursion continues to **P.S.1, a public school that has been transformed into the world's largest contemporary art center.** In P.S.1, itself a happening, the playground, classrooms, hallways, gymnasium, even stairwells—with retro graffiti intact—are the galleries. (**Monday is a good choice for your Queens excursion since most museums elsewhere are closed then.**)

A short ride from midtown on the **#7 local** train takes you to **MoMA QNS** (33rd St. and Queens Boulevard; 1-212-708-9400; Th-M 10-5; F-10-7:45/contr. after 4PM; $8.50-12). A modern movement to Queens occurred literally on June 23, 2000, when precious icons—pivotal works in the development of modern art—were transported here from MoMA, Manhattan in a village-like saint's day procession. As a brass band played and devotees strewed rose petals, paintings and sculptures were carried aloft into heavy traffic, around barriers, along detours, up, onto and across the Queensborough Bridge. The video of the event, "**Modern Procession,**" is on view here along with mixed media, interactive programs, and the provocative visiting exhibits New Yorkers expect of MoMA. There is a snackbar on the second level near the celebrated **Design Store**. But with good restaurants en route today, you may decide to delay lunch.

To reach the **Museum for African Art,**(36-01 43rd Ave. at 36th St.; 1-718-784-7700; $3-6; M/T/F 10-5; S/S 11-6), walk up Queens Blvd. to 36th St.; turn left to 43rd Ave. The collection has the portrait masks, Madonnas and equestrian figures, assemblages, ritual objects, royal bronzes and regalia that changed the course of Western art. Curators and staff are genuinely concerned with education. Exhibits speak effectively to—not down to—children. The bright and beautifully appointed warehouse space is temporary until a permanent site is available on Manhattan's Museum Mile. Avoid the crowd; come to Queens.

Hungry Now Or Later? Find **a variety of restaurants on Queens Blvd.** at 39th and 40th Sts. Choices include Italian **Dazies** (#39–41; 1-718-786-7013); Turkish **Hemsin**, (#39–19; 1-718-482-7998), and the moderately priced Romanian **Harmony** (#39–23), with its *mittel Europa* feeling. The **P.S.1 Café** is in an artist designed setting. Nearbye **Mannettas** (45th Ave.) has brick oven pizza.

After a snack or lunch, take the #7 local at 33 St. back towards Manhattan to the 45th Road-Court House Square station for **P.S.1 Contemporary Art Center** (22–25 Jackson and 46th Ave.; 1-718-784-2084; Th-M 1-6; cl.T/W; $2–5). Check out the rest rooms; they may be installations; climb the stairs to the top floor gymnasium to see monumental works, appropriate to the astounding space. P.S.1 endeavors to connect artists, curators, patrons, and audiences. All of these art folks party here on occasion, in the tradition of the grand *beaux arts* balls. Call for information. Near P.S.1, a stroll on **45th Avenue** is a particular treat **between 11th and 21st Sts., where landmark brownstones predominate and there are several good restaurants.**

Directions For MoMA QNS, #7 local train from Times Square, 5th Ave., or Grand Central to 33rd St. and Queens Blvd. station. To P.S.1, #7 train in the direction of Manhattan to 45 Road-Court House Square station. A **Queens Artlink shuttle bus** departs hourly on weekends from East 59th street between Park and Lexington Aves. and makes a continual loop between sites.

Want To Know More Websites are africanart.org; and moma.org; ps1.org. For a comprehensive reference, see "Theories of Modern Art: A Source Book by Artists and Critics," Herschel P. Chipp (1996)

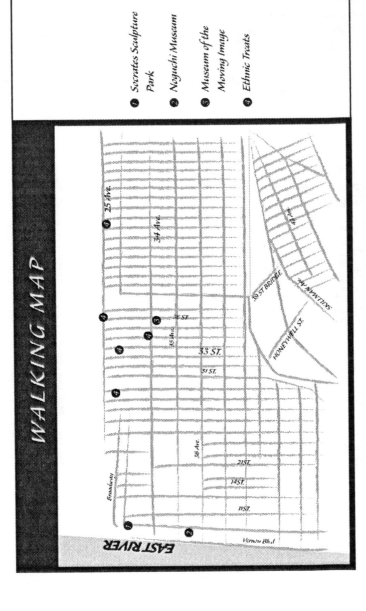

WALKING MAP

EAST RIVER

1. Socrates Sculpture Park
2. Noguchi Museum
3. Museum of the Moving Image
4. Ethnic Treats

Astoria's Secrets

The Noguchi Museum, the Socrates Sculpture Garden and Ethnic Treats

Astoria's secret is no more. Word is out on this lively Queens neighborhood fronting the East River, easily accessible by subway, with great views of the city's skyline. Our day's highlights are two unusual art sites, **Socrates Sculpture Park** and **Isamu Noguchi's Garden Museum**, and a wide choice of interesting **ethnic restaurants** for lunch or dinner after the art.

At the edge of the East River, with a fabulous view of the Manhattan skyline, is **Socrates Sculpture Park** (1-718-956-1819; open daily daylight hours; free). At the intersection of Broadway and Vernon St., the four acre Park, formerly a marine terminal, is now the outdoor setting for large scale abstract and figurative works in stone, metal, and found materials. Having languished for over a decade as a modest sculpture space, the park was about to be displaced by luxury condos, when the community, some politicians and Mark di Suvero, an internationally known creator of enormous steel sculptures, worked together to make the space a permanent art park. The sculptures are witty and whimsical, such as one that portrays urban street life through figures of hip hop youths; another is a carousel of found objects.

Just a few blocks away is **The Noguchi Garden Museum** (32–37 Vernon Blvd., 1-718-204-7088; W/Sat/Sun 11-6; $5 donation/seniors $2.50; best visited between Apr-Nov; call for hours as these change seasonally. The museum is under renovation and has moved to Long Island City until 2003). Designed by the world-renowned sculptor, Isamu Noguchi himself, it contains more than 250 pieces in a lovely indoor/outdoor setting symbolizing Noguchi's Japanese and American cultural heritage (his ashes are buried in both Japan and the United States). The museum stands in charming contrast to the largely industrial and commercial neighborhood which surrounds it, a spot Noguchi chose in the 1960s to be near his stone suppliers and obtain a large affordable space. The sculptures, with their rough and smooth textures; the museum building with its large windows; and the garden, with its Japanese influences, reflect the integration of East and West in Noguchi's life. Here the visitor becomes familiar with Noguchi's lifetime work of shaping earth, water, sound, space and light into sculptures utilizing a wide variety of media—stone, clay, wood, and metal. Two films in the museum focus on Noguchi's versatile career—he created everything from public environments such as playgrounds, bridges, and fountains to extraordinary stage sets for modern dancer Martha Graham. A free "walking guide" and an excellent catalogue are available. Allow two hours for this special site.

Hungry? After all this art has whetted your appetite, feast on some of Astoria's excellent ethnic food. Astoria emerged from its history as a 19th century resort for the wealthy (it is named after John Jacob Astor) to the most ethnically diverse zip code in the country; in the late 19th century it was the home of mainly Greek immigrants and today also contains large numbers of immigrants from Central and Latin America, Pakistan, and the Middle East. This diversity has resulted in great choices for ethnic food, much of it found in a 6 square block area about 8 blocks from Noguchi. Many of the Greek restaurants, such as **S'Agapo** (34–21 34th Ave; 1-718-626-0303; daily noon-3; 5:30 on) and **Stamatis** (31–14 Broadway; 1-718-204-8964; noon-1AM), are standouts for grilled fish. **Omonia Cafe** (32–20 Broadway/33rd St.; 1-718-274-6650; open 24 hours) is a MUST for its fabulous desserts; at **Taverna Zenon** (34–10 31st Ave.; 1-718-956-0133; T-Sun lunch/dinner) the food is Cypriot Greek and the adjacent bakery features super delicious yoghurt berry cakes. Also nearby is the Latin American **Tierras Colombiana** (33–01 Broadway/33rd St.; lunch daily from 11AM; 1-718-426-8868).

If you have time after lunch, the **American Museum of the Moving Image** (35th Ave. at 36th St., 1-718-784-0077; T/W/Th 11-5; F noon-5; Sat/Sun 11-6; $10; seniors/students $7.50) is a great place for film buffs, and everyone will enjoy **Red Grooms' Tut's Fever Movie Palace** with its classic serial films, and the chance to use the interactive video, animation, computer generated, and audio technology. If you don't have time to visit it today, plan a return trip and combine it with some other great **ethnic** restaurants such as the Greek **Esperides** (37–01 30th Ave at 37th St.; lunch daily noon-3; 1-718-545-1494), the Egyptian **Mombar's** (25–22 Steinway St., 1-718-726-2356; T-Sun 5-midnight); or the authentic Thai **Ubol's Kitchen** (24–42 Steinway St./25th Ave., 1-718545-2874; lunch/dinner), less than a mile away on or near Steinway St., a very interesting and typically multicultural Queens thoroughfare.

Directions For Socrates Park from midtown Manhattan, N train towards Queens to the Broadway station; leaving the station, head straight ahead (west) on Broadway for the river, 8 blocks away (you can also take the Broadway Bus #104). To the Noguchi Museum, turn right when you exit Socrates Park (past the COSTCO); it's just a few blocks away. You can reach the restaurants from Noguchi by walking back the way you came (or taking the same #104 Bus) up Broadway to 31st Street and locating the addresses of your restaurant of choice. Depending on where you eat, return to Manhattan by the N train either at Broadway (the stop you exited) or at 30th Avenue. Or, if you've visited the Museum of the Moving Image or S'Agapo, take the R train at the Steinway St. station.

Want To Know More About Noguchi? Ian Buruma, "Back to the Future," NYReview of Books, March 4, 1999; Dore Ashton, "Noguchi: East and West" (1992). "Isamu Noguchi and Modern Japanese Ceramics," Louise A. Cort and Bert Winther-Tamaki.

WALKING MAP

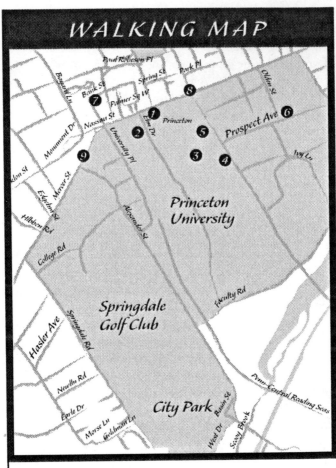

- ❶ Maclean House
- ❷ Alexander Hall
- ❸ University Art Museum
- ❹ Frist Campus Center
- ❺ University Chapel
- ❻ Eating Clubs
- ❼ Palmer House
- ❽ Bainbridge House
- ❾ Albert Einstein's House

Town and Gown

A Day in the Ivy at Princeton, New Jersey

F. Scott Fitzgerald called Princeton "paradise"; this beautiful university setting certainly has elysian elements that invite discovery on a one-day outing from New York. Serpentine paths on the rolling **campus** wind through a labyrinth of ivy-covered neo-Gothic buildings, stone archways and landscaped gardens. The excellent **University Art Museum** is open to the public as is the graceful **University Chapel. Stately mansions** that were once exclusive **eating clubs** (akin to fraternities) line Prospect Avenue. These clubs are probably not what Groucho Marx had in mind when he said he'd never join an association that would accept him; indeed elitism here was such that until the democratizing 1960s, Albert Einstein, the most important of scholars associated with the university, might not have gotten a bid. The campus faces **Palmer Square,** the commercial center of the **revolutionary town,** within walking distance of gracious historic houses, boutiques, crafts shops, student cafes, and good restaurants.

Take **New Jersey Transit** (1-201-7622-5100), Northeast Corridor Line, from Pennsylvania Station for the one-hour trip to Princeton Station. A 9:38 train is suggested for a full day excursion. At Princeton Junction, transfer to the one car "dinky" to complete the trip to the Princeton University campus. Walk from the depot north towards the entrance gate on Nassau St. Pass campus landmark, **Alexander Hall,** a solid neo-Romanesque structure with rounded walls, turrets, and a carved façade. Nearby, at the security booth, pick up a map. Just inside of the campus gate, **Maclean House** (1-609-452-3603) offers tours, maps, and information.

Visit **the University Art Museum** (1-609-258-3788; T-Sun; cl. M and holidays; free/donation; gallery talks), a short walk south (away from Nassau St.) in McCormack Hall. In front of the museum is a very **large Picasso sculpture**. The museum's collections of eastern and western art, which span the centuries from antiquity to modernity, are a pleasure for the public as well as a valuable resource for art history students and visiting scholars. Alumnae gifts enrich the museum's holdings and may reveal a benefactor's intriguing idiosyncrasies. The Greek vases with scenes of domestic life are enchanting. Especially appealing, too, are the African headdresses and Chinese coffin panels. The painting galleries are outstanding.

Hungry Now Or Later? For lunch or a coffee break with students, the **Frist Campus Center**, a modern building just southwest of the museum, through the Prospect Gardens, offers good, huge deli sandwiches. To dine alfresco, try sitting outside on a wall. Choices for **a lunch in town** include **Old World Pizza** (242 Nassau St). The **Annex Grill** (128 Nassau) has ample inexpensive Italian. **Quilty's** is a French bistro at 18 Witherspoon St., (perpendicular to Nassau Street; 1-609-683-4771). **Olive"s Gourmet Bakery and Deli** (22 Witherspoon St.) serves lunch as does the **Yankee Doodle Tap Room** in the famous **Nassau Inn** (center of **Palmer Square**).

From the **Frist Campus Center**, a short walk north and then west takes you along the stretch of **Prospect Avenue** where the legendary eating clubs are located. Afterwards, return to the **University Chapel** (Washington Road, behind the school of Architecture; afternoon concert series). The **stained glass—designed by American artists**—is truly unique. Brilliant windows depict Princetonians who were advocates for religious freedom such as John Witherspoon, sixth president of the college and the only clergyman to sign "The Declaration of Independence." Engraved text on the pulpit reads, *"An* *instructed democracy is the surest foundation of government; and education and freedom are the only sources of true greatness and happiness among any people.* If you wish to spend more time on the campus, walk south, cross Faculty Road to **Carnegie Lake,** where the sculling team practices. It is open to the public for canoeing, boating, ice skating,and picnicking.

Going to town? Cross Nassau St. into **Palmer Square,** the commercial center. **Bainbridge House** (158 Nassau St.; 1-609-921-6748) is home to **The Princeton Historical Society.** This 1776 Georgian brick house has changing exhibits, a library, and photo archive. **Albert Einstein** lived at **112 Mercer St.,** a western extension of Nassau Street.

Directions Buy a rt ticket at New Jersey Transit in Penn. Station. Website is njtransit.com. Busses to Princeton leave from Port Authority Bus Terminal (1-212-LO4-8484).

By car: Princeton is at the junctions of Rte. 206 and Rte 27, a few miles west of Rte 1, which goes straight across New Jersey. The Turnpike is near; take exit 8 onto 571 West directly onto the campus.

Want To Know More? F. Scott Fitzgerald's "This Side of Paradise" (1920), called by some "the most influential American novel of its time" is set in Princeton. For information and to reserve tickets to special events and performances: 1-609-452-3000; website: princetonartmuseum.org

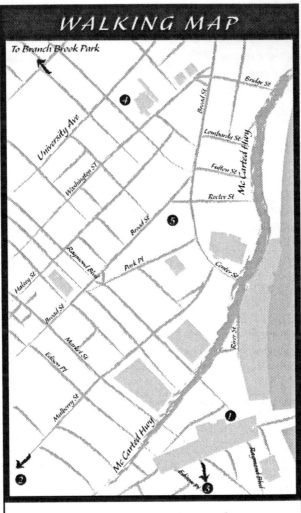

WALKING MAP

To Branch Brook Park

University Ave

Washington St

Bridge St

Broad St

Lombardy St

Fulton St

Mc Carter Hwy

Rector St

Broad St

Raymond Blvd

Park Pl

Center St

Halsey St

Broad St

Market St

River St

Edison Pl

Mulberry St

Mc Carter Hwy

Raymond Blvd

① Penn Station   **④** The Newark Museum

② Priory Jazz Club   **⑤** Military Park

③ Ferry St. Restaurants

PATHways to Art and Music
Newark, New Jersey

Newark, New Jersey is an easy trip by PATH from New York City, and a great place to spend a day, especially a Sunday, when you can take advantage of a unique **jazz brunch**. Newark is the site of the first class **Newark Museum**, noted for its American and Tibetan collections, and interesting **historic buildings and parks**. It also has many **ethnic restaurants**, so plan this day with brunch or lunch in mind.

Founded in 1666 as an agricultural settlement, Newark became a major transportation and manufacturing hub by the 19th century and retained that prominence until just after World War II. Newark's working and middle class Jewish population then moved to suburbia—many from the Weequaic section, immortalized in the novels of Philip Roth. By the 1960s Newark was sliding downhill, but it reemerged in the 1990s as a dynamic "must see" city. Building on its long jazz tradition— Newark's WBGO (88.3 FM; www.wbgo.org.) is the only "all jazz all the time" station in the metropolitan area and the best continuous jazz station in the country—Newark now boasts the exciting New Jersey Performing Arts Center (1 Center St.; 1-888 466 5722), with its excellent Theatre Square Grill. And if you go in mid-April, you're in for a cherry blossom treat in Branch Brook Park that's hard to match anywhere (see Special Events).

Newark's appeal is evident as soon as you exit the PATH train from New York into the beautiful Art-Deco **Penn Station** that unlike Manhattan's, managed to survive the 1960s destruction of so many historic urban buildings. Spend a few moments admiring the building (which also has a Newark information center) before you exit the station.

Hungry? Your **Newark Sunday** starts with great food and music in the unique church setting of **The Priory Restaurant and Jazz Club** (233 West Market St.; 1-973 242 8012; **jazz brunch** Sun 11-3; $16; Jazz also Fri, Sat, Sun 7 pm; check information for the correct bus and leave by the Market St. exit of Penn Station, or take a taxi).

As an alternative to the jazz brunch, on Sundays, or during the week, there are many **ethnic restaurants** on **Ferry Street**, heart of the **Ironbound District** named for the freight railway tracks (now disused) that form its borders. Leave Penn Station at the Ferry St. exit; the restaurants are about a 20 minute walk on this main street lined with Portuguese and Brazilian restaurants, supermarkets, and bakeries. The Ironbound is also serviced by the Loop Bus, which stops in front of Penn Station.

The Ironbound District has a heavy concentration of Portuguese, Cuban and other Spanish-speaking residents, who support the neighborhood's many ethnic stores and restaurants. Until the 1960s, the area was dominated by Polish, Italian and Spanish immigrants; at that time the poverty of Portugal under the dictator Antonio Salazar led to an exodus of many Portuguese.

While that immigration has slowed with the improvement of the Portuguese economy under its more liberal government, Brazilians, attracted by their shared language, and Ecuadoreans, Columbians and Mexicans, have been filling the gap. The Latino flavor of the Ironbound is most apparent in its **Ferry St. restaurants**, such as **Fornos of Spain** (47 Ferry St.; 1-973-589-4767; daily lunch from 11:30); **Vila Nova do Sol Mar** (263 Ferry St.; 1-973-344-8540; daily lunch); and **Casa Nova** (262 Ferry St.; 1-973-817-8712; daily lunch from 11AM; weekends from noon). Also check out the excellent Portuguese bakeries such as Coutenho's, Delicias, Averrense, and Padaria Brazileira.

After the food and the music, the next stop on this special day is **The Newark Museum** (49 Washington St., 1-973-596-6550, W-Sun noon-5, cl. holidays, sugg. Adm. $2-5; fee parking). From The Priory, take a taxi; from the Ironbound you can walk back to Penn Station and take the LOOP Bus, or walk from Penn Station; it's about 1.5 miles. This flagship museum of New Jersey is located in a neo-classic structure with spacious rooms, high ceilings, and a very inviting courtyard café (the site of many free musical performances). It contains a rich American collection, and among its world famous **Tibetan collection** is a complete Buddhist altar. The "must see" **Ballantine House**, a Victorian confection is located just behind the museum's main building.

After the museum, it's a lovely walk back to Penn Station via **Washington Park,** down Broad St. to the adjacent **Military Park,** dotted with monumental, historical sculptures including those of George Washington, Christopher Columbus, and "The Indian and the Puritan."

Directions By train: PATH trains to Newark leave from 33rd St., 23rd St., 14th St. or 9th St.in Manhattan; $1.50 fare; bring $1 and $5 bills for the machine. There may be a same platform change at Hoboken or Journal Square.

By car: Holland Tunnel from Lower Manhattan to NJ Turnpike, Exit 15W to 280 West. Take the Newark exit marked *Downtown/Arts District.*

Want To Know More? The many novels of Philip Roth: "Portnoy's Complaint," "Goodbye Columbus," "American Pastoral" and others, take place in this section of New Jersey. See also the New Jersey Historical Society, 52 Park Place (1-973-596-8500; T-Sat 10–5 for tours and exhibits).

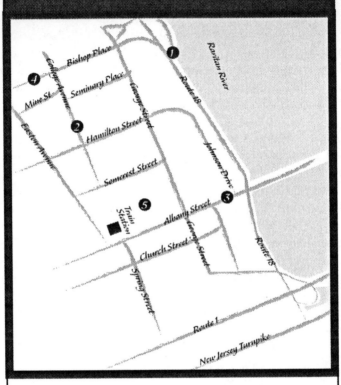

WALKING MAP

❶ Rutgers Display Gardens   **❹** Rutgers Campus

❷ Zimmerli Museum   **❺** New Brunswick

❸ Albany St. Restaurants   Train Stration

ROAMING in RUTGERS

Rutgers University Display Garden and the Zimmerli Art Museum

In 1869, Rutgers defeated Princeton in the first formal college football game. **The Rutgers University New Brunswick campus** is a splendid site for a perfect day combining walks in nature and the excellent **Zimmerli Art Museum**. (If you drive, you can do the whole day, but public transportation can take you to the verdant Rutgers campus, the Museum and New Brunswick eateries very easily).

The little-known **Rutgers Display Gardens and Helyar Woods** (near U.S. 1 and Rte 18; daily, dawn-dusk; no charge; 1-732-932-8451), 50 acres on the Raritan River, is a delightful spot containing both diverse planting in formal garden settings and shady forests. Flowering shrubs bloom from late April to June and annuals mid-June through September. Fall colors glow on trees and shrubs September through October. The Helyar Woods offers lovely, easy walks on marked trails through old growth forests and along the Raritan River.

Hungry? Save lunch for New Brunswick, only a 15 minute drive away; these good restaurants in downtown New Brunswick are within walking distance of the Rutgers campus and the Zimmerli Museum. The **Old Bay Restaurant** is across the street from the Hyatt Hotel on Albany St.(reservations suggested; 1-732-246-3111; M-F 11:30-3, Sat/Sun dinner only); another good choice is **Old Man Rafferty** (126 Albany St., daily

11:30–3); and the Museum itself has a delightful indoor/outdoor café with light lunches.

The Jane Voorhees Zimmerli Art Museum (called The Zimmerli; 71 Hamilton St., New Brunswick; 1-732-932-7237, www.zimmerlimuseum.rutgers.edu; T-Fri 10:00–4:30; weekends noon-5:00, cl.Mondays and some holidays; $3) is part of Rutgers University. Its permanent collection includes American and French paintings, Japonisme, historical Russian art and a very special and fascinating collection of **Soviet underground art**. This collection, a gift of Norton and Nancy Dodge, is a vast historical record of a cultural movement that may evoke some negative aesthetic reaction, but never fails to provoke reflection on the relationship between art and politics.

Directions (By car, train or bus, about 1 hr). By car to Rutgers Display Gardens: N.J. Turnpike (Rte 95) from the Holland Tunnel, south to Exit 9, to 18 N. to Rte 1 S, to Exit "Ryders Lane towards E. Brunswick." Take the first left turn (it comes very quickly) to Log Cabin Road, to the Farm; free parking. To the Museum from the Gardens, return to Ryder Road, turn right to Rte 1 N., to 18 N to 27 S., take a quick right turn on Johnson Ave. to George St.; 2 hour metered parking in front of the museum and nearby. If you are driving directly to the Museum: NJ Turnpike to Exit 9, follow signs for Route 18 North, for about 3 miles. Follow large overhead green sign that reads "George Street, Rutgers University, Exit ½ mile." At the exit light (George St.) turn left. Go to the next traffic light at Hamilton St.; the Museum is on the right corner. To return to Manhattan continue up George St. to the first light, turn right. At the second light (at end of street), turn right, go about 2 miles and follow the signs for the NJ Turnpike.

By public transportation: The Suburban Transit Bus to New Brunswick leaves from Port Authority (1-800-222-0492). By train: NJ Transit to New Brunswick leaves from Penn Station (1-800-626-7433 for fare and schedule). For lunch on Albany St. before your museum visit, walk downstairs from the train station to Albany St.; the restaurants are just a few blocks away (you'll pass Nielson St. on your right where you turn for the Museum).

Want to Know More? "New Art from the Soviet Union: the Known and the Unknown" Norton Dodge and Alison Hilton (1977); "Socialist Realist Painting," Matthew Brown (1998).

WALKING MAP

❶ The Bruce Museum	❺ Greenwich Avenue
❷ Greenwich Harbor	

Awaken Your Senses on the Sound

The Bruce Museum and Greenwich, Connecticut

The lovely New England town of **Greenwich, Connecticut,** only an hour away from midtown Manhattan, is a pleasant visit in all seasons. The jewel in the Greenwich crown is the **Bruce Museum of Arts and Science,** located at the crest of a hill that overlooks the **town harbor.** In 1908, Robert Bruce, a textile manufacturer, bequeathed the Victorian mansion that houses the museum to the town, with the stipulation that it become a public museum. The building was redesigned in a classic spare art-deco style in the 1930s. Visiting shows of **fine and decorative arts** are displayed with uncommon finesse. The permanent collection offers select **American Impressionists.** Children have a lot to do in a touchy-feely room, crafts workshop and large outdoor playground. An **eastern woodlands diorama** depicts early spring 500 years ago on the Sound. The museum co-sponsors **nature and flower walks** in conjunction with the Connecticut Botanical Society. **Greenwich Harbor** is a scenic seascape; **Greenwich Avenue** contends with Rodeo Drive in Beverly Hills and Worth Avenue in Palm Beach for posh shops, bistros, cafes, and elegant restaurants.

The Metro-North Train, Harlem Line, leaves Grand Central Station for Greenwich Metro-North Station at short intervals during the day. A 10A.M. departure will allow time for a leisurely contemplative day, beginning with the **Bruce Museum of Arts and Science** (1 Museum Drive; 1-203-869-0376; T-Sat 10–5; Sun 1–5; $5). The museum is a short walk south of the station. Walk down the hill. Turn at street level onto **Steamboat Road;** continue along under an overpass to a traffic light; turn left, and as you round the hill, two life-like dinosaurs and a totem pole signal your arrival at the Bruce.

Hungry? Bruce Museum cafe may be booked by a private group. Just outside, **Bruce Park** is perfect for picnicking. Greenwich has fine possibilities for strolling and for dining. Greenwich Harbor is to the left of the railroad station, along Steamboat Road. For a very pleasant seafood lunch, on a patio overlooking the harbor, try the **Atlantis Restaurant** in the **Greenwich Harbor Inn** (500 Steamboat Road; 1-203-661-9800). **Maneros** (559 Steamboat Road;1-203-869-0049) is a popular family steakhouse. For sophisticated ambience, walk to **Greenwich Avenue,** which is below the station at the foot of the hill. **Thataway** (#409) has good burgers and wraps. **A stretch of serious shopping and other eateries is straight ahead.**

Directions Travel rt from Grand Central Station to Greenwich on Metro-North (1-212-532-4900) Harlem Line.

By car, take I 95, exit 3, at Arch St.or the Merritt Pkwy, exit 3, at North St.

Want To Know More? Website: brucemuseum.org. "Greenwich" (2000), by Howard Fast, who lives there. See "American Impressionism, 2nd ed." by Jane R. Becker (2001).

City Beats

WALKING MAP

Bronx Zoo

1 Lexington Ave. Subway Exit

2 Asia Gate Zoo Entrance

3 Southern Blvd. Gate Exit

4 187th St. Belmont Neighborhood

5 Arthur Ave. Market and Dominick's Restaraunt

6 Fordham Rd. busses to subways

The Unbeatable Bronx

The Bronx Zoo and Arthur Avenue

In the "golden age" of the post-war Bronx, visiting the **Bronx Zoo** and eating a hearty meal at Dominick's Restaurant on **Arthur Avenue in the Italian enclave of Belmont**, was a weekend ritual. Although the rising affluence of the 50s and the social changes of the 60s emptied much of the Bronx of its middle class, Belmont remained little changed. Although the neighborhood has always had a small African American and Hispanic population, and now includes more recent Serbian and Albanian immigrants, its character is still marked largely by the culture of Bari, Italy, the home of many of its first immigrants. Today, a number of Arthur Avenue's younger generation have returned to this neighborly enclave to continue family businesses. The **dining and food shopping** at the vibrant **Indoor Retail Market** (busiest on Sat; closed Sun) and neighborhood restaurants are exceptional (see Special Events, August). The **Bronx Zoo**, a ½ mile walk from Arthur Avenue, has probably altered more than Belmont—from a standard animal park into an outstanding conservation facility that invites somber reflection on the state of our planet along with delight in the antics of our feathered and furry friends. November and December visits offer fabulous **animal illuminations** (see Special Events, December), while late Spring and Summer celebrate the adorable **animal babies.**

Start this perfect Bronx day at the **Asia Gate of the Zoo** (1-718-220-5100; open daily 10–4:30; $6, W free; cafeterias, shuttle bus to major areas), by taking the #2/#5 train to E.180th St. (Boston

Rd./E. Tremont Ave.) station. Exit the subway, turn right and keep on the right for the short walk up 180th St. Worth a moment's view is the **West Farms Old Soldiers' Cemetery**, with its graves of veterans from the War of 1812, the Civil War, the Spanish American War and WWI. The name "West Farms" reflects the area's 18th century rural origins when both large plantations using slave labor, as well as modest farms, exported grain, timber and livestock to the West Indies as part of the growing sugar economy.

Beyond River Park on the Bronx River, a large sign 3 blocks to the right beckons you to the **Zoo's Asia Gate.** Obtain a zoo map to plan your visit, by foot or shuttle, with the **Southern Boulevard Gate** as your ultimate destination. One of our favorite zoo sections is the new **Congo Gorilla Forest** ($3), with its surprise-ending film! You can keep on past the Southern Boulevard Gate for the showy **Birds**, the **Children's Zoo** (Apr-Oct), and the remarkable **Fountain Circle Main Gate** with its towering Rainey Memorial bronze sculpture adorned with 22 full size animals. But return to the Southern Blvd. Gate for your exit.

Hungry? Hope so. A short walk brings you to great eats in **Belmont**. After exiting the Zoo, cross over the street. At the first traffic light turn right, walk to E. 187th St. and turn left. A few blocks down E. 187th is the Belmont veteran, **Artusa Pastry Shop** (670 E. 187th St.) with its delicious cannoli, tiramisu, homemade Italian ice, and other tempting desserts. At 2348 Arthur Ave. is the **Madonia Brothers Bakery**, a family-run shop for over 88 years especially recommended for its super-fresh *semifreddo* (cream) cannolis. If you're planning to eat your lunch at the renowned Dominick's Restaurant a few blocks away, you can take pastries from these shops for your dessert there, as Dominick's permits you to bring your own. At **Arthur Avenue**, turn left to reach the neighborhood magnet at #2344: the **Indoor Retail Market** (Mon-Sat til 5:30), established by Mayor Fiorello LaGuardia to get the pushcarts and street vendors off the avenue. Pack up some tasty cheeses and cold cuts (at prices lower than Manhattan's) for home consumption. If you're going to skip a restaurant dinner, there's delicious pizza and pastas at the **Cafe Al Mercato** and fabulous *schiaccata,* open vegetable sandwiches at **Mike's Deli** inside the Market. For a major meal, join the crowd (especially packed on weekends) at the fabled **Dominick's** (2335 Arthur Ave.; 1-718-733-2807; no reservations, **cash only**), whose unpretentious atmosphere and huge portions of top quality food have made it a city-wide favorite for nearly a century. As you stroll around Arthur Avenue to enjoy the street life, note the flyers and store placards in Serbian and Albanian; neighborhood residents from these homelands have opened some raffish cafes with authentic food and atmosphere to match.

Directions To the Bronx Zoo's Asia Gate take the #2/5 train to the E. 180th St. (Boston Rd./E. Tremont Ave.) station. To go directly to Arthur Avenue, take the B/D or #4 train to Fordham Rd., then the Bx12 bus to Hoffman St. To return from Arthur Ave., walk to E. 190th St./E. Fordham Rd. and cross over for the Bx12 bus (every 10 minutes) to the Valentine Avenue D train subway entrance. For the Lexington Ave. subway, do not cross E. Fordham Rd., but take a short right to the bus stop for the Bx12 bus going the opposite way.

By car: Take the Bronx River Parkway, Exit 6 and circle the Zoo for the Asia Gate parking lot. For Belmont area parking, drive from the Zoo parking lot to E. 187th St. and Belmont Ave.; there's metered parking and a nearby public lot.

Want To Know More? Zoo Website www.wcs.org Browse the Gift Shop for books about the Zoo. Films with Belmont-like settings include "A Bronx Tale" (1993) and "Marty" (1955). See George Fluhr's "The Bronx Through the Years: A Geography and History (1964), Gerald Rosen's "Growing Up Bronx" (1984) and Herman Wouk's classic novel "City Boy: The Adventures of Herbert Bookbinder" (1969). Also see Will Eisner's remarkable comic book tales about the Depression-era Bronx, "A Contract with God and Other Tenement Stories" (1978).

WALKING MAP

16th St.
Windsor

Prospect Ave
Prospect Expwy
17th St
18th St

4th Ave
5th Ave
21st St
22nd St
24th St

25th St
26th St
27th St

① (Gatehouse Entrance to Greenwood)

ens Expwy
28th St
29th St
30th St
31st St
32nd St
33rd St
34th St
35th St

Green-wood Cemetary

2nd
Belt Parkway
4th Ave
60th St
61st St

② Pier 69
Senator St
65th St
66th St

Bay Ridge Ave
63rd St
64th St

70th St
71st St
4th Ave

③ Shore Road
Shore Rd
Narrows Ave
Colonial Rd

Bay Ridge Parkway
Ovington Ave
72nd St
74th St

Bay Ridge

Belt Parkway
Harbor Ln

77th St
78th St
5th Ave
6th Ave
7th Ave
Brooklyn Queens Expressway

3rd Ave
4th Ave
79th St
80th St
81st St
82nd St

Bay R
77th St
78th St
79th St
80th St

④ Century 21

85th St
86th St
87th St
88th St
89th St
90th St
91st St
92nd St
93rd St
94th St

Oliver St

Ridge Blvd

Colonial Ave
n Pkwy
To Bridge

83rd St
84th St
85th St
86th St
87th St
10th Ave
11th Ave

---

① Gatehouse Entrance to Greenwood

② Pier 69

③ Shore Road to Verrazano

④ Century 21

Stayin' Alive!
19th Century to Century 21
Green-wood Cemetery and Bay Ridge, Brooklyn

Green-wood Cemetery (1840) in Brooklyn is a beautiful, if a bit bizarr-o, Victorian necropolis. The first burial was in 1848; you may glimpse the most recent burial on your visit today. Through the 19th century until the opening of Prospect Park, Green-wood provided a bucolic respite for city folks from the steadily increasing urban clamor. Families picnicked, couples courted, and children frolicked amidst tombstones and classically embellished marble mausoleums. Green-wood continues to be inviting year round and is unusually dramatic in Autumn, when the thickened black tree trunks that line winding paths are crowned with flamboyant gold and crimson foliage. Today's excursion extends to **Bay Ridge,** which is accessible from Green-wood by bus and subway. Bay Ridge turns the southwest corner of Brooklyn; the "ridge" overlooks the narrows, the entrance to New York Harbor. **Shore Parkway** offers **walkers and cyclists** an exquisite harbor view especially at sunset. Originally a Dutch colonial settlement, dating to the 1600s, Bay Ridge eventually became a Norwegian enclave and still has vestiges of Scandinavian culture. Today, it is known for **cultural diversity, cafes and good restaurants of all stripes, and great shopping**. Christmas lighting displays draw people from all parts of the city. (See Special Events, December).

To begin, take the R train to 25th St. station in Brooklyn and walk 1 block east to **Green-wood Cemetery** (500 25th Street; 1-718-768-7300). The stunning entrance, a **gatehouse complemented by two triumphal arches** is considered the very best surviving example of the New York Gothic Revival style. Stroll the 478 acres of hills, ponds, and landscaped areas on your own or **join a tour. Call ahead for times and specific meeting places** (1-718-469-5277; Sun, beginning at 1PM; $6). Our dour docent, the W.C. Fields of walking guides, provided us with informative bits such as a list of countless famous folk who are *not* buried in Green-wood. Some who *are,* are Currier and Ives, "Boss" Tweed, Harry Houdini, and Alice Roosevelt. Alice's cousin, Eleanor Roosevelt, was fond of reading and ruminating besides the mournful ivory angels at Alice's grave. A nearby tombstone reads "Sick and Tired of Being Sick and Tired."

To continue to **Bay Ridge,** return to the R train. Exit the train at 68th St./Bay Ridge Ave.station. You now have two possible walking routes. One is directly **to the waterfront** and then south along Shore Parkway to 86th St., and even beyond to the Verrazano Bridge at 95th St. To reach the **waterfront**, walk east on 69th St.,which is also Bay Ridge Avenue, **to Pier 69,** a promontory for seeing the entire Bay, the Verrazano Bridge, Staten Island, and the lower Manhattan skyline. **The alternate route** is south through city streets from 69th St along 3rd Ave. to 86th St. The stretch through town on and near to 3rd Ave. is fine for **shopping, strolling, and, of course, dining**. Interesting shops along the way include **Things on Third** (7920 3rd) for cool Brooklyn souvenirs. For crafts, see **All By Hand** (8415 3rd). **Kleinfeld**, the famous bridal wear emporium, is at 8206 5th Avenue; **Century 21** is at 472 86th St.

Hungry Now And Later? For take-out and take-home, **Mideast Bakery** (7803 3rd Avenue) has oven-fresh specialties. Traditional **Scandinavian** treats are yours in **Nordic Delicacies** (6903 3rd Avenue) and **Lesky's Bakery** (7612 5th Avenue) **Choc-Oh! Plus** (7911 5th Avenue) is for chocolate lovers and chocolate bakers; further south, **Hinsch's** (8518 5th Avenue) is an **ice cream parlor/luncheonette**.

Good choices for restaurants on 3rd Avenue begin with **unique divine pizza**: **Nino's** (#9110), **Lento's** (#7003), **Del Corso's** (7002), and **Vesuvius** (#7303). **Soup as Art** (#8321) is owned by Soprano's actor Joseph Gannascoli. Latin **Sancho's** (#7410; 1-718-0070) is a locals' favorite for dinner only. **Skinflint's** (7902 5th Avenue) has good plentiful **pub grub**. Two exceptional, upscale restaurants require reservations: Greek **Ellia** (8611 3rd. Avenue; 1-718-748-98) and **Tuscany Grill** (8620 3rd Avenue;1-718-921-56330), which will save you the trip to Florence.

Directions For Green-wood Cemetery, take the R train to the 25 St. stop in Brooklyn. To continue to Bay Ridge, take the R train to 68th St. (Bay Ridge Avenue stop). The B37 Bus makes the same trip on 3rd Avenue, but traffic may be heavy. Return to Manhattan via the R train from 86th St.. **Express busses**, X27 and X28, leave from 86th St for Union Square and midtown Manhattan.

Want To Know More? "The City of the Dead and Other Poems," Andrew Dickenson (1845); "Brooklyn's Green-Wood Cemetery: New York's Buried Treasure," Jeffrey Richman (1999) and the cemetary website: green-woodcom for tours. For free birding tours, call John Borker, 1-718-875-6212. "Bay Ridge," is by Lawrence Stelter (2001). "Saturday Night Fever," starring John Travolta, with music by the Beegees was set in Bensonhurst, but filmed in Bay Ridge.

WALKING MAP

Harlem River

St. Nicholas

Fred Douglass Blvd.

W. 144th St.
W. 143rd St.
W. 141th St.
W. 139th St.
W. 138th St.
W. 135th St.
W. 134th St.
W. 133rd St.
W. 132nd St.
W. 131st St.

1b

1a

W. 130th St.
W. 129th St.
W. 128th St.
W. 127th St.
W. 126th St.
W. 125th St.
W. 124th St.

W. 132nd St.
W. 131st St.

2

3

5

Lenox Avenue

W. 123rd St.
W. 122nd St.
W. 121st St.

W. 127th St.

W. 126th St.

Lexington Ave.

6

W. 120th St.
W. 119th St.
W. 118th St.
W. 117th St.
W. 116th St.
W. 115th St.

W. 123rd St.
W. 123rd St.
W. 121st St.

1c

4

1a - **1c** Harlem Churches

2 Sylvia's Restaurant

3 Park Historic District

4 Shabazz Open Air Market

5 Amy Ruth's Restaraunt

A Great Day in Harlem
Gospel, Soul Food and Historic Architecture

One hot August day in 1958, photographer Art Kane took a photograph of over 50 American jazz greats crowded onto a brownstone stoop at 17 E. 126th St. in Harlem. Later published in *Esquire,* this remarkable photograph, emblematic of Harlem's spirit and style in good times and bad, became renowned as "**a great day in Harlem.**" On today's "great day in Harlem" you'll hear some of the **church gospel** and inspired preaching that has nourished African Americans for centuries, enjoy a "poor people's" cuisine that turned meagre resources into tasty, filling **soul food**, and walk down the wide avenues and legendary side streets of the **Mount Morris Park Historic District** filled with **architectural treasures.** At the end of your day you can browse through the lively **Malcolm Shabazz Open Air Market's stalls** of Afro-centered clothing and artifacts. There's too much of Harlem to be done in one day, but after one journey "uptown," you'll surely want to return.

Harlem is a wonderful place to visit **on a Sunday,** when neighborhood **church services** offer a warm welcome to both tour groups and independent visitors. (Dress modestly, try for an aisle seat in case you do not stay for the entire service, and be sure to drop a contribution [$5 suggested] into the collection plate). Services may vary in length from 1 to 3 hours and may include not only rousing **gospel music** and a sermon, but other congregational activities as well. These services are not performances: the **glorious voices** and **inspired preaching** are integral to the profound spiritual beliefs of the congregants. Attending a service will illuminate the historical and continuing centrality of religion in the African American community. Simone Weil, the French philosopher who fled to New York to escape the Nazis, found her greatest solace in the churches of Harlem.

Start your **Sunday in Harlem** with a hearty breakfast, as lunch could come late. One welcoming church is the neo-Gothic **Metropolitan Baptist** (151 W. 128th St. at Adam Clayton Powell Jr. Blvd.; 1-212-663-8990; #2/3 train to125th St., walk 3 blocks north, then west), founded by a former slave. The service begins around 10:45; late entrants are courteously seated; and the full service, which may take up to 3 hours (you'll be handed a pamphlet about it) is very moving for its sincerity, musical accompaniments, charismatic preaching and congregant participation. Another Harlem church that welcomes visitors is **Abyssinian Baptist** (136 W.138th St. between Adam Clayton Powell Jr. and Malcolm X Blvds.; 1-212-862-7474; C train to 135th, walk 3 blocks north, then east), whose fame spread with the reputation of its powerful, flamboyant preacher (later Congressman) Adam Clayton Powell Jr. Services begin around 10:45, with music by the outstanding Chancel Choir.

(You can **reverse the order of your day in Harlem** by starting with the service at a third Harlem church, **Memorial Baptist, 141 W. 115th St.** between Lenox and St. Nicholas Aves.;1-212-663-8830; 1-212-663-8830; #2/3 train to 116th St., which has restructured its service for visitors, with the gospel music taking place mostly between 11 and noon. Then you can **lunch** at **Amy Ruth's** [113 W. 116th St.], renowned for its ribs, shrimp dishes and cobblers or at one of the tiny African eateries that have sprung up among the mosques and halal stores here such as **Keur Sokhna** [225 W. 116th St.] or **Africa Restaurant #1** [247 W. 116th St.]). After a visit the **Shabazz Market**, you can complete your day with the **Mount Morris Park Historic District walk** [see these below, and return from 125th St.])

Hungry? If you've attended a service on 128th or 138th St., there are several good luncheon choices south along Lenox Avenue. **Mannas** (486 Lenox/134th St.) offers a delicious buffet of Southern style food in a casual setting (as do two other similar eateries: Manna's Soul Food & Salad Bar at 2331-3 Frederick Douglass Blvd./125th and Manna's at 51 E. 125th/Park). A few blocks further down Lenox at 126th St. is the justifiably famous family-owned **Sylvia's** (328 Lenox; 1-212-996-0660), which is often jammed on Sundays—when it offers intermittent gospel singing—with large parties and tourist groups. However, you may get a vacant seat at the counter along with the locals or you may want to return on a weekday to savour its huge portions of authentic Southern cooking. A pleasant Sunday alternative is the new **Bayou** (308 Lenox/125th St.;1-212-426-3800), which serves delicious Creole luncheons in its attractive second floor dining room.

Harlem during the week also allows you to attend a **gospel service**, or, if you prefer, a gospel concert. **Mt. Moriah Church** (2050 Fifth Ave. at 127th St.; 1-212-289-9488; #2/3 or #4/5 trains to 125th St., walk west to 5th Ave. and 2 blocks north) has a **Wednesday morning** service for its Addicts Rehabilitation Center with a marvelous choir (11AM; tell the doorkeeper you would like to attend the service and make a donation; service is 1½ hours.) **Friday nights** there are gospel concerts; call to check the schedule. In addition to the Harlem restaurants mentioned above, **weekday lunches** with delicious, inexpensive African American style food in a pleasant setting are available at the **Windows Over Harlem Restaurant in the Harlem State Office Building** (163 W. 125th St. 3rd fl.; 1-212-665-4337; picture ID required; lunch until 4:00; **happy hour with live entertainment 5–8PM**).

Now it's time to **walk off that lunch** and enjoy some of the **architectural treasures** of Harlem. As its name indicates, Harlem was first settled by the Dutch. In the 17th century it was a fishing village on the East River. Eventually the community spread west into the heights of upper Manhattan (see The ABC's of Upper Manhattan), and by the 18th century the area between 120th and 160th Sts. was dotted with the country estates of the wealthy. By the mid 1800s, many of these were converted into farmland: one elderly black man interviewed for a local history spoke of searching for farm work in Harlem as late as 1907. The 1850s and '60s saw the area decay into a wasteland of squatters and wandering domestic animals. But after 1873 when Harlem merged into New York City, the swamps were drained, elegant rows of brownstones and institutional buildings were erected, and increased transportation attracted a white middle class, including a large population of European Jews. Much of Harlem's fine architecture dates from this period.

Developers overbuilt, however, and turn-of-the-century recessions left many stately homes and institutional buildings empty, a magnet for black residents and the growing congregations of black churches squeezed into decaying areas of mid-Manhattan. As African Americans moved in, more affluent whites started moving out to the boroughs. By the end of WWI, with the Great Migration from the south and the Harlem Renaissance of the 1920s, the area became the vibrant mecca and symbol of black America.

The blocks off Lenox Ave. south from 135th St. to 120th St. still contain many distinctive buildings from the last decades of the 19th century. On 130th St. east to Fifth Ave. are the 1880s **Astor Row houses,** low brick, single-family homes with decorative wooden porches and large front and side yards reminiscent of Southern domestic style. On commercial **125th St.** the architecture is not the draw, but there are two Harlem landmarks of interest. A few blocks west is the **Theresa Hotel** (2090 Adam Clayton Powell Blvd.; now an office building), where Fidel Castro made his historic speech before the U.S. closed off Cuba to Americans. At 253 W. 125th is the newly restored **Apollo Theater,** which once hosted such performers as Duke Ellington and Billie Holiday, but where inept performers on

Wednesday "amateur nights" were yanked off the stage with a shepherd's crook.

Back on **Lenox Ave.** at 125th is the start of the **Mt. Morris Park Historic District** walk. Thread your way between Lenox Ave. and Mt. Morris Park W. St., noting the century-old religious institutions that give Harlem so much of its character: **Commandment Keepers Ethiopian Hebrew Congregation** (NW corner of 123rd St. and Mt. Morris Park W), originally the home of the founder of Arm and Hammer baking soda—which suggests the wealth once found here—and now the temple of a congregation of black Jews; the Romanesque confection of **Mt. Morris Ascension Presbyterian Church** (16–20 Mt. Morris Park W., corner 122nd St.; **St. Martin's Episcopal Church** (18 W. 122nd St., corner of Lenox) whose bulky tower houses the city's second largest carillon of 40 bells; the twin-turreted **Ebenezer Gospel Tabernacle** (225 Lenox, corner of 121st St.), originally a Unitarian church, then a synagogue; the austere neoclassic **Mt. Olivet Baptist Church** (201 Lenox Ave, corner W. 120th), originally a prestigious German Jewish temple. On a clear afternoon, detour into **Mt. Morris (now Marcus Garvey) Park** at 121st St. to ascend the unique cast-iron Fire Watchtower with its 10,000 pound bell for a broad overview of Harlem.

On Lenox Ave., continue downtown to **Malcolm Shabazz Open Air Market** on 116th St. off 5th Ave. (1-212-987-8131; open daily 10AM–8:30 PM), for a unique shopping experience. If you want to take a bit of Harlem home with you, sample the fabulous fresh-fried fish goodies at **Sea and Sea** (next door to the market) before boarding your subway home.

Directions Harlem sites and restaurants noted in the day are accessible by #2/3 trains as indicated in connection with the sites. Return from 116th St. via #1 train at 5th Ave or #2–3 at Malcolm X Blvd stations.

Want To Know More? The Schomburg Center for Research in Black Culture (515 Lenox Ave./136th St.; 1-212-491-2200; cl. Th and Sun; open Sat 10-5; weekdays noon-5; occasional exhibits) is renowned for its collection; for purchasing books, visit The Liberation Bookstore (Lenox at 131st St; 1-212-281-4615). See the "AIA Guide to New York City" sections on Harlem and the Heights. The New York Landmarks Conservancy (141 5th Ave. NYC 10010) publishes "Touring Historic Harlem," 4 walking tours of the area. The documentary "A Great Day in Harlem," produced by Jean Bach, is a must for jazz lovers. The Studio Museum in Harlem (144 W. 125th St.; 1-212-864-4500) and the National Black Theatre (2031 5th Ave. at 125th St.; 1-212-722-3800) are two well-known Harlem institutions. Literature by Harlem writers such as Langston Hughes, James Baldwin and Claude Brown abound; see also analytic studies such as John L. Jackson Jr.'s "Harlemworld: Doing Race and Class in Contemporary Black America" (2002) and Monique Taylor's "Harlem Between Heaven and Hell" (2000); crime fiction such as Chester Himes' famous "Cotton Comes to Harlem" (1965) series; and photograph collections such as James Haskins "James Van Der Zee, the Picture-Takin' Man," (1979). A fascinating study of African street vendors is "Money Has No Smell: The Africanization of New York City," Paul Stoller (2002).

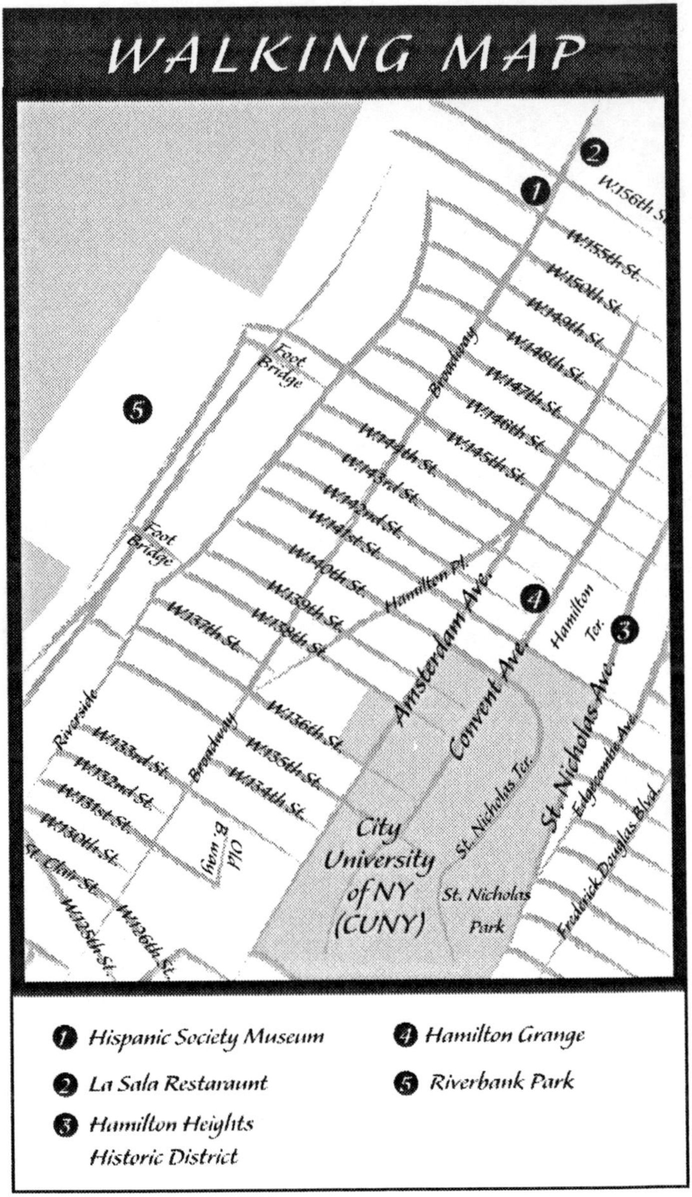
WALKING MAP
W.156th St
W.155th St.
W.150th St.
W.149th St.
W.148th St.
W.147th St.
W.146th St.
W.145th St.
W.144th St.
W.143rd St.
W.142nd St.
W.141st St.
W.140th St.
W.139th St.
W.138th St.
W.137th St.
W.136th St.
W.135th St.
W.134th St.
W.133rd St.
W.132nd St.
W.131st St.
W.130th St.
St. Clair St.
W.125th St.
W.126th St.
Foot Bridge
Foot Bridge
Broadway
Broadway
Old B.way
Riverside
Hamilton Pl.
Amsterdam Ave.
Convent Ave.
Hamilton Ter.
St. Nicholas Ave.
Edgecombe Ave.
Frederick Douglas Blvd.
St. Nicholas Ter.
St. Nicholas Park
City University of NY (CUNY)
1 Hispanic Society Museum
2 La Sala Restaraunt
3 Hamilton Heights Historic District
4 Hamilton Grange
5 Riverbank Park

The ABC's of Upper Manhattan

Architecture in Hamilton Heights, Beauty in the Hispanic Society and the "Countryside" of Riverbank Park

Today's excursion—a Friday or Saturday is required to access all the sites on one day—highlights **Hamilton Heights**, a surprising storehouse of art, architecture and history on the hilly upper West Side from 155th to 135th Sts. Resting on the granite escarpment thrusting up from the Hudson, is the block-long square of the **Hispanic Society of America**, sometimes called the city's best little-known museum. It offers a profusion of paintings, sculpture and cultural items that delight the mind and the eye, as well as a wonderful gift shop. The **Hamilton Heights Historic District**, once called Sugar Hill for the "sweet life" of its African American residents, is an architectural fantasy, with each row house on these picturesque streets different from its neighbors. Nestled among these 19th century beauties is the **Hamilton Grange**, the summer home of Alexander Hamilton, from whose balcony on the Heights this devoted New Yorker had spectacular views to the Hudson. Now a small museum, its enthusiastic ranger guide brings one of New York's first citizens and his times to life. Just a few blocks away, with the river visible from the hills of Convent and Amsterdam Avenues, is one of the city's newest green spaces, **Riverbank Park**, a hive of neighborhood activities from outdoor weddings to rollerskating to quilting workshops.

The #1 train to Broadway and 157th St. takes you right to the **Hispanic Society of America Museum**, where Goyas, El Grecos, and Valesquezes rub shoulders with antique maps, textiles and ceramics of the Iberian peninsula, Latin America and the Philippines (Bway between 155th and 156th St.; 1-212-926-2234; T-Sat 10–4:30; Sun 1–4; call for holiday closings; free).

Hungry? Museum staff recommend **La Sala** (3750 Bway at 156th; 7AM-11PM), a tiny restaurant with hearty "comida" in the Latin style. Similar restaurants are sprinkled down Bway and its side streets en route to the Hamilton Heights Historic District at 144th St. A new entry is **Mexico Dos Corp.** (1726 Amsterdam Ave./145th St.; 1-212-234-3334; daily 8AM-midnight). Also in the area is **Copelands** (549 W. 145th/near Bway; 1-212-234-2357), a Harlem institution renowned for its soul food buffets (somewhat pricier than in the past).

From bustling, commercial Broadway, turn east at 144th St. for 1 block to the **Hamilton Heights Historic District**, once part of Alexander Hamilton's estate. Thread your way east to the dead end of 144th and Hamilton Terrace and around Convent Ave. from 144th to 140th Sts, where a glorious mix of restored Gothic, Tudor, Flemish and Romanesque row houses meets your eye. Planned as a neighborhood for the well-to-do at the turn of the century, when the area became accessible by the "el," the streets declined after WWI. The 1930s saw many of the homes bought up by African Americans. Three CCNY professors. Three important churches, adjacent City College and the **Hamilton Grange** are linchpins of this truly unique district.

The **Hamilton Grange National Memorial** (Convent Ave. between W. 141st and 142nd Sts.; 1-212-283-5154; F-Sun 9–5, free; tours hourly [may be undergoing reconstruction shortly]), Alexander Hamilton's "country" home celebrates the life of this outstanding immigrant from the West Indies. A contributer to every aspect of the city's political, economic and social wellbeing, Hamilton patronized local artisans and merchants to furnish his home. But he only had two years to enjoy retirement on this estate, with its gorgeous Hudson views and unique architectural features. His antagonism to Aaron Burr's election as his adopted state's governor provoked the duel that ended his life. Ask the ranger for the fascinating details of this rivalry, Hamilton's extra-marital affair and subsequent blackmail—which only proved his financial impeccability—and his ambivalence about dueling, which caused not one but two family tragedies.

Retrace your steps to 145th St. and Broadway; then descend the heights for some "country in the city" at **Riverbank State Park** (Cultural Complex: 1-212-694-3634; Athletic Complex:1-212-694-3636). **Spectacular Hudson River views** on two levels, as well as a variety of recreational pleasures, await in all seasons. You'll want to return again and again.

Directions To Hispanic Society, #1 train to 157th St.; walk 2 blocks south. Walk or take the Bway bus down to Hamilton Heights (or access the Heights separately by #1 train to 137th St.; then walk 2 blocks north and east to Convent Ave. The #1 to 145th St. and a few blocks walk west takes you directly to Riverbank Park.

Want To Know More? "AIA Guide To New York City" (Hamilton Heights). "If I Should Die: a Mali Anderson Mystery" is one of several *policiers* by Grace F. Edwards set in the Hamilton Heights area. A standard biography of Alexander Hamilton is Broadus Mitchell's "Alexander Hamilton" (1957–62); see also Ron Chernow, "Alexander Hamilton" (2003).

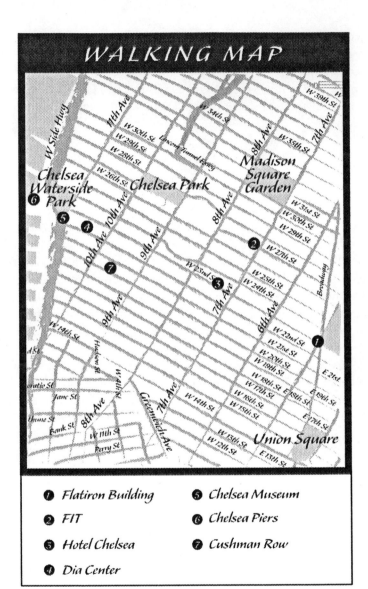

WALKING MAP

Chelsea Waterside Park

Chelsea Park

Madison Square Garden

Union Square

● Flatiron Building

② FIT

③ Hotel Chelsea

④ Dia Center

⑤ Chelsea Museum

⑥ Chelsea Piers

⑦ Cushman Row

Chic to Cheek in Charming Chelsea

The Flatiron Building, Fashion Institute Museum, Avant-garde Art Galleries and the Chelsea Piers

Chelsea is for free spirits: Chelsea is for artists and models, for writers and actors, for singles, for partners, and for families. This full day excursion offers a sampler of its ample and uncommon charms. Major sites on or near the W. 23rd St. route include the landmark **Flatiron Building,** *la tres chic* **Museum at the Fashion Institute of Technology (FIT)**, the Victorian Gothic **Hotel Chelsea, Dia Center for the Arts**, selected galleries packed with vanguard painting, photography and sculpture. Final destination is the **Chelsea Piers, a** mammoth sports complex, where residents build endurance and hone muscle, particularly the *glutial maximus* which shows to advantage in the form fitting outfits they buy in neighborhood boutiques. Parks and restored brick and brownstone townhouses make the area a city walker's delight, but the M 23 bus crosses Chelsea's historic and artistic center, saving energy for all there is to see and do.

Begin on 23rd St. where Broadway and 5th Avenue cross at **The Flatiron Building** (1902), a freestanding triangular skyscraper (175 5th Ave.). In 1902, Chicago architect Daniel H. Burnham wrapped the Flatiron's slender silhouette in the rusticated limestone façade of a Renaissance palazzo, thereby suggesting an analogy between New York's newly powerful industrialists and the mighty patrons of the 15th century Italian city states. Paradoxically, the building's importance to architecture is its strong steel frame skeleton—the structural innovation that would make possible New York's signature 20th century skyline.

Walk up 5th Ave. to **Tannen's Magic Shop** (24 W. 25St.; 2nd fl., 1-212-929-4500) which appeals to those with an interest in the occult. Clerks may give demonstrations. Continue uptown to the recently renovated fire engine red **Gershwin Hotel** (7 E. 27St.). Built in the roaring1920s, gigantic flame-like ornaments appropriately spiral up the façade; inside, the lobby welcomes visitors with artwork on every wall.

Walk west to **The Museum at Fashion Institute of Technology/FIT** (27th St. between 7th/8th Aves; 1-212-217-5800; T-F 12–8; Sat 10–5; free). FIT, a division of the State University of New York/SUNY, is among the best endowed colleges in America thanks to the largesse of those highly successful alumni whose famous labels are worn on the outside. Theatrical, joyful exhibits are brilliant reminders that fashion is indeed art. A recent Bill Mackey retrospective featured the designer's interpretation of Scarlett O'Hara's gown made from the living room draperies in the novel "Gone With the Wind." The "Mackey," a creation designed for a Carole Burnette spoof of the great film, had a broomstick through the shoulders.

Now, the route turns south, back to 23rd St. Beneath tiers of richly ornamented wrought iron balconies, enter the **Hotel Chelsea** (222 W.23rd St.), where artists and writers, famous and infamous, have lived and worked since the 1890s. For some tenants, the artistic struggle has necessitated a donation—in lieu of cash—to the hotel management; hence, the very valuable lobby décor.

Hungry Now Or Later? East of 8th is close, just E. of 8th Ave. on 23rd St.; **Intermezzo** has returned to 8th Ave. between 20th and 21st Sts. **The Lunch Basket** (403 W. 24 th St. between 9th and 10th Aves.; breakfast till 1PM) has organic everything. Find good Italian at **Pepe Giallo to Go** (253 10th Aves. between

24th and 25th Sts.) Small, spare, and zen, **Wild Lily Tea Room** is far west (511A 22nd St.); the menu is far-east with representative teas from everywhere.

Garages and warehouses converted into multi-level art galleries line 23rd, 22nd and 21st Sts. near 10th Ave. These places are imposing, but the doors open, the elevators work, and there is rarely an admission fee. A site where the space within matters more than the façade without is the **Paula Cooper Gallery** (535 W. 21st St.). The cheeky art scene actually laughs at itself in **Comme Des Garcons** (520 West 22nd St.; 1-212-604-9200), a pretend clothing store peddling an imaginary clothing line. (Later, you might visit **Gene London,** an actual retail store peddling real vintage theatrical clothing (897 Broadway at 20th St., 5th fl.; 11–6). Also on 22nd St. is the highly regarded **Dia Center for The Arts** (#548; 1-212-989-5566; W—Sun12–6;$6); weather permitting, see the "park" on the roof. **Chelsea Art Museum** (#556; 1-212-255-0719; W-S noon-6; $5) is new, bright and stimulating.

Our Chelsea sampler has variety. The small houses that line the streets remind visitors of its very pretty small town flavor. **Cushman Row** (406–418 W.20th St. between 9th and 10th Aves.) is beautifully preserved. Notice that cast iron pineapples, symbols of hospitality, adorn many stoops. These may have been the homes of 19th century sea captains whose tall ships were moored close by on the Hudson. Traditionally, real pineapples, placed on doorsteps, signaled a ship's return from an exotic place and were an invitation to celebrate by partaking in the literal fruits of the crew's labors.

Continue west to **Chelsea Piers** where giant 20th century luxury liners once berthed (waterfront between 17th/23rd Sts.; 1-212-336-6666). Find pedestrian access at 23rd St. Restored and revitalized in 1994 as a vast sports complex, each of four piers has places to play (basketball, bowling, and ice skating, for example) and to dine—always with a harbor view and fresh sea breeze. Listen to live music on summer weekends. If you are inclined to do more than stroll, shop, have a brew or a meal, call ahead for sports and performance schedules: Sky Rink 1-212-336-6100; Golf Club 1-212-336-6400; Origins Spa 1-212-336-6780; Sports Center 1-212-336-6000; Roller Rinks 1-212 336-6200; Spirit Cruises 1-212-727-2789; Maritime Center 1-212-336 SURF.

Directions N/R to 23rd and 5th Ave.station to start; #1/9 to 28th St. station for FIT. The nearest stop to Chelsea Piers is the C/E train to 23rd St./8 th Ave. station; the M23 bus crosses 23 St. all the way to the Chelsea Piers.

Want To Know More? "The Flatiron": A Photographic History of the World's First Steel Frame Skyscraper 1901–1990," Peter Gwillion Kreitler (1991). Many scenes in the film "Sid and Nancy" were shot in the Chelsea Hotel. Websites: fitnyc.edu/museum and chelseaartmuseum.org

WALKING MAP

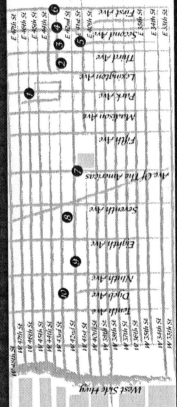

1. Grand Central Terminal
2. Chrysler Building
3. Pfizer Headquarters
4. Ford Foundation
5. Daily News Building
6. The United Nations
7. New York Public Library
8. Times Square
9. Port Authority Bus Terminal
10. Ford Shops

Fabulous Forty-Second Street

Walking River to River

This fascinating **river-to-river walk** pays homage to all the things that make New York City great—commerce, industry, knowledge, the arts, and especially the energy and diversity of its people. The 2-mile route (you can hop a bus part way through) takes most of the day but there are many eating and resting places (and restrooms) along the way. The walk begins at **Grand Central Terminal**, proceeds **east to the East River** and then turns around **west** all the way to the **Hudson River**.

This perfect day starts at the newly renovated, awe-inspiring **Grand Central Terminal**, the Beaux-Arts structure built by "Commodore" Cornelius Vanderbilt 70 years ago when he joined 36 railroad lines into the New York Central. After exiting from the 42nd St. subway station (called Grand Central Terminal), cross 42nd St. to the Pershing Bridge to view the awesome sculpture group of Hercules, Mercury and Minerva above the Tiffany glass clock (accurate to within seconds) high at the Terminal's entrance. Cross back inside the expansive **main concourse** to **look up** at the vaulted ceiling's replication of the sailor's sky. (By mistake, the artist painted the constellations of the zodiac backwards, as a mirror image, but "Commodore" Vanderbilt—part of his fortune was made in shipping—was too frugal to pay for repainting, so he claimed the designs were depicted as they would appear from outer space, or as seen by God, rather than man).

Hungry? Downstairs in the Terminal, adjacent to the Grand Central Market is the Food Court and the famous **Oyster Bar** (shellfish priced by the piece, $1.50–$2.00). Near the Oyster Bar, at the four marble columns that form a square, you may see people who appear to be talking to themselves, or into hidden telephones. No hidden phones—these are the "**whispering columns**": if you whisper into one of their corner joints, you can be clearly heard by a person listening at the diagonally opposite column.

To the left of the columns is **The Campbell Apartment: Cocktails from Another Era.** Formerly an actual New York "studio" apartment of the 1920s (and later the Terminal's Police Station and jail), it has been remodeled as a lounge serving wine ($8 a glass) daily after 3PM, to those wearing "proper attire," a description of which is posted at the lounge entrance.

Upon exiting the Terminal on 42nd St. and continuing east, you'll find the Grand Hyatt Hotel, whose elegant marble lobby contains a waterfall and hundreds of banked fresh flowers. Pause to look across the street at the classic Art Deco facade of the **Chanin Building** (122 E. 42nd St.). Continuing east, stop at the **Chrysler Building** (135 E. 42nd St.), one of New York's best-loved landmarks. Its Art Deco facade includes "gargoyles" made of shiny radiator caps from a 1929 Chrysler, and a frieze of wheels with radiator caps girdles the structure. Inside, in the marble lobby, **look up** at one of the world's largest murals, depicting transportation and human endeavors, which includes an image of the building itself at the Lexington Avenue entrance. Influenced by the Egyptian craze of the era, the elevator doors are modeled after the tomb of King Tutankhamen and each elevator interior has a different Art Deco design.

Exiting the Chrysler Building at 42nd St., continue walking east (left) toward 3rd Avenue, until you reach **Pfizer Headquarters** (235 E. 42nd St.) whose lobby wall mosaic is a fascinating depiction of multicultural healing procedures (obtain a free brochure identifying the mosaic's elements at the reception room just beyond the security desk). Two blocks further on (between 2nd and 1st Avenues) you can enter the **Ford Foundation Building** which boasts a beautiful indoor garden.

As you continue walking east you'll pass **Tudor City**, a self-contained "city within a city" in Tudor Gothic style. Its adjacent parks (up the staircase) provide serene bowers for taking a breather. At the corner of 42nd St. and 1st Avenue, **Ralph Bunche Park** honors the United State's first African American UN official, who was awarded the Nobel Peace Prize in 1950. With its inscribed hope for peace on the north wall, the park is the backdrop for many international human rights demonstrations. (Here you may want to detour left to the **United Nations** Secretariat Building at 1st Avenue and 45th St. In addition to an inviting outdoor sculpture garden with artworks donated by UN members, a tour center and small art exhibits on UN themes, there is also a snack bar, an outstanding gift shop and the UN post office. The Delegate's Dining Room is open to the public for early lunch, 11:30-2:30 weekdays; reservations suggested; 1-212-963-7625).

To start your walk west, cross 42nd St. and 1st Ave; **look ahead** for a photogenic view of the top of the Chrysler Building. At 2nd Avenue the old **New York Daily News Building** (220 E. 42nd St., now TV Channel 11) displays in its lobby the **world's largest interior globe,** indicating Earth's position relative to the other planets. To save your feet a little, you may now want to take the 42nd St. crosstown bus to the New York Public Library at 5th Avenue. Walkers **continue west,** and take a closer look at the Art Deco facade and lobby of the **Chanin Building** (at Lexington Avenue). Two blocks further on, just before Madison Avenue, is the Whitney Museum of American Art at Philip Morris, a one-room gallery in a restful atrium (with benches and a restroom).

The next stop is the the **Forty Second Street Library,** a gorgeous Beaux-Arts building whose front steps on 5th Ave. are guarded by its famous pair of lions. In the early 19th century the site was a potter's field; in the mid-19th century the Croton Aqueduct, which provided the city's water supply, occupied this spot. A high walled promenade called Reservoir Square surmounted the block, providing a popular area for city strollers. In 1899 the reservoir was demolished to make way for the new Library (for more information on the Library see Quiet Gems of Midtown Manhattan).

Hungry? **The Terrace Cafe** overlooking 5th Ave. in front of the Library boasts "the best sandwiches in New York City" and **The Bryant Park Grill**, just behind the Library in **Bryant Park** (named for orator, journalist and poet, William Cullen Bryant) is excellent for a more leisurely (and more expensive) lunch. Tourists resting their tired feet share the shady expanse of the Park's lawn with construction workers eating lunch, bocce and domino players, and Library and office workers from nearby buildings on their breaks. (Coffee and snack bars, tables, chairs and benches are available throughout the park; there are clean public restrooms are on the 42nd St. park side just west of 5th Ave. adjacent to the subway stop and also inside the Library.) Bryant Park, like many city greens, deteriorated greatly in the 1970s, but a successful renovation by a joint government and private conservancy has brought it back to life. It hosts many film and music events in Summer.

Continue walking west across 6th Ave. (renamed Avenue of the Americas by New York's feisty mayor Fiorello La Guardia, but still called 6th Ave. by New Yorkers); the unsightly block from here to Times Square exemplifies the "bad old days" before **Times Square** was renovated. The famous intersection of 42nd St., Broadway and 7th Ave. (officially Times Square runs along Broadway from 42nd to 51st Street) is the entrance to the Great White Way, the greatest theatre district in the world. The Times Square clean-up is still debated: some New Yorkers think it's been oversanitized into a Disney-like theme park, but its glitz and glitter still make it a "must-see" for every visitor. By city law, 18% of the signage on Times Square must be kinetic! The former Times

Tower (One Times Square), still attracts hundreds of thousands of New Yorkers and visitors on New Years Eve to await the midnight lowering of the famous illuminated sphere.

Walking west on 42nd St., past Broadway, you pass the **New Amsterdam Theatre** (home of the Lion King), whose opulent reconstructed Art Nouveau interior can be viewed on a one hour tour ($10). Across the street is the New Victory Theatre, a successful Times Square renovation for moderately priced and innovative multicultural performances oriented toward families.

You'll next pass the new Madame Tussaud's Wax Museum ($20 for adults, 1½ hours). A few doors down, **look up** at the entrance to the Times Square Hilton for the witty signature bronze sculptures "Time and Money" by Tom Otterness. His satirical New York scenes continue inside the lower lobby and in the Sky Lobby (on the 4th floor), where you can join two of Otterness's figures raising a glass in Celebration, at the Lobby Bar.

At 42nd St. and 8th Ave., inside the 8th Ave. entrance to the **Port Authority Bus Terminal**, is the entrancing audio-kinetic sculpture "42nd St. Ballroom" by George Rhoads. (In the main waiting area of the south wing, to the left, is George Segal's sculptural grouping "Commuters.") Like so much of New York, the Bus Terminal, once a tawdry place known for its high crime rate, has been transformed, to the great pleasure of its transportation customers and visitors alike. And you won't be "bowling alone" if you have a game on its newly jazzed up second floor bowling alley, one of the few left in Manhattan (2nd level, 9th Ave., 1-212-451-0495; open daily, 10AM-11PM).

Exiting the Terminal, look diagonally ahead to 9th Ave, where the 25 story Manhattan Plaza buildings provide federally subsidized housing for performing artists, whose presence has been essential in revitalizing the area. Between 9th and 10th Avenues there are several upscale restaurants and a raft of small "off-Broadway" theatres, an important part of the Times Square restoration.

Two blocks more and you're at the **Hudson River**. But this great walk ain't over yet! You can now take the 42nd St. crosstown bus back east to the subways, BUT, if you have just a little energy left, there are some delicious taste treats ahead. At 10th Ave. turn left to 43rd St, then right. On 43rd St., between 10th and 9th Aves., under the stone arcade, you'll find two wonderful dessert stops, to eat in or for take-away: **The Little Pie Company** (424 W. 43rd) and **Good and Plenty to Go** (410 W. 43rd St.). And ahead, on 9th Ave., one block north on 44th St., there are fresh-baked Greek pastries at the **Poseidan Bakery** (629 9th Ave.) to take home. Indulge yourself—you deserve it!

Directions The walk begins with your exit from the Lexington Avenue IRT subway #4/5/6 train in Grand Central Terminal. The walk ends on the west side at the Hudson River. You can take the 42nd St. crosstown bus back to 8th Ave. subway (A, E, and C trains), to the N/R train at Broadway, or to the Shuttle at 7th Avenue to Grand Central Terminal for the east side trains.

Want To Know More? For a return visit, check out the **free tours** at Grand Central Terminal, every Friday 12:30; meet across the street in the Whitney Museum Atrium. The United Nations daily 45 minute tours are on the hour; 1-212 963-8687. Free Times Square tours go every Friday, 12:30 from the Visitor Center at Broadway and 47th St. Books about 42nd St. include "Grand Central Terminal: Railroads, Engineering, and Architecture in New York City," Kurt C. Schlichting (2001); "Down 42nd Street: Sex, Money, Culture, and Politics at the Crossroads of the World," Marc Eliot (2001); and "Times Square Roulette: Remaking the City Icon," Lynn B. Sagalyn (2001). The Broadway show and film "42nd St." celebrates this unique thoroughfare.

WALKING MAP

E. 10th St.
E. 8th St.
E. 4th St.
Bleecker St.
Houston St.
Spring St.
Delancey Street
Prince St.
Grand St.
Chambers St.
Fulton St.
John St.
Manhattan Bridge
Brooklyn Bridge

① Grand St.
② East River Park
③ Exit into East Village
④ St. Mark's Place
⑤ Tenement Museum
⑥ Chinese Foot Massage
⑦ Subway from Chinatown

The Sidewalks of New York
The Grand Street Circle

For more than 100 years, "nature" and recreation for the "huddled masses" of Manhattan's Lower East Side meant swimming in or walking along the East River, sunning in the tiny parks and gardens squeezed around tenements, enjoying the inexpensive cultural activities of community churches, synagogues or settlement houses, shopping in small locally owned stores and clubbing in ethnically-oriented neighborhood eateries. Much of this community-generated social life still remains, as this leisurely, 3-mile circular Grand Street excursion illuminates. From **Grand Street** via the **East River Walkway,** you'll enter the **East Village,** then circle down to **Orchard Street for bargain shopping** and a visit to the remarkable **Lower East Side Tenement Museum.** Back on Grand Street, a **Chinese foot massage** completes the day.

After exiting the Grand Street subway station just east of the Bowery, walk east on **Grand Street,** the "grand" thoroughfare formed by filling in the "stinking sewer" of the paradoxically named Fresh Water Pond in the early 1800's. First a center for working class theatres and circuses, Grand St. in the mid to late 1800s became the site of Irish and Italian Catholic churches; by the turn of the century it housed many Jewish textile and linen establishments, and, today, it is home to many small Chinese-oriented businesses. The modern Henry Street Settlement at 466 Grand is a famed and still active reminder of the Settlement House movement for the early immigrants. At the revered **Kossars,** (367 Grand), you can cross the road for some bialys to take home. This unique European *kuchen* is still baked here under orthodox Jewish regulations that sacrifice part of the dough "for the priests" and offer a blessing on each new batch. At 313 Grand, a Jewish Ritualarium (*mikvah,* or ritual bath) continues to serve the neighborhood's large Orthodox Jewish population. Across the street again, are New York's first "projects," the Hillman Houses, named for labor leader Sidney Hillman, whose words on a bronze plaque encapsulate the cooperative idealism of the early days of public housing.

Use the green-bannistered overpass on your left, in the shadows of the gigantic stanchions of the Williamsburg Bridge, to access the **East River walkway.** The East River, where immigrant children (including the authors' fathers) used to swim is not actually a river, but a salt water estuary of the Bronx's North River. Here, indeed, is the city-as-island: comorants diving for fish, a surprising variety of water traffic, contrasting views of the low-rise Polish neighborhood of Greenpoint, Brooklyn (actually a part of Long Island) across the river, midtown Manhattan's dramatic skyline, and Roosevelt Island plopped down in the middle.

At 10th St., just past the basketball courts, the **East Village** is entered via the overpass. This is **Alphabet City** (Aves. D, C, B and A), once notorious for its high crime rate, but now a cohesive community with a welter of small, funky boutiques and eateries and many renovated, architecturally interesting tenements. Community wall paintings (Ave. C between 9th and 10th Sts.), neighborhood gardens (Ave. B at 10th St. and at 12th St.); and institutions that have served the immigrants for a century (the decorative St. Nicholas Carpatho-Russian Orthodox Church at 10 St./Ave. A; the Russian/Turkish Baths on 10th St./1st Ave., a (now modernized) reminder of the days when most Lower East Siders didn't have private bathrooms; and the Episcopalian St. Mark's Church in the Bowery on 10th St./2nd Ave, known for its New Year's Day poetry readings (see Special Events, January) and its lovely meditation garden, proclaim the heterogeneous ethnic and social mix of the neighborhood:

blacks, whites, and Latinos, young families and oldtimers, working people and NYU students. Your ultimate goal for a respite
and lunch is **St. Mark's Place at 8th St.** (between 2nd and 3rd
Aves.), the hippie era "mall," still going strong after 35 years.

Hungry? St. Mark's Place offers many charming and inex-
pensive venues for a light or full lunch. Highly recommended is
La Palapa Cocina Mexicana (77 St. Mark's Pl. between 1st/2nd
Aves.). **Indian Restaurant Row on 6th St. between 3rd and 1st
Aves.** offers a vast array of that subcontinent's cuisines and is
especially recommended for vegetarians.

To complete your East Village walk, drop into the glorious
Ukrainian craft shop **Surma** (11 7th St., ½ block east of 3rd
Ave.) and note St. George's Ukrainian Catholic Church, both
testifying to the specific immigrant heritage of this street.

Continue walking south on 3rd Ave. to Houston St., cross
over and turn left (east) for the few blocks to **Orchard Street's
Tenement Museum** (90 Orchard; 1-212-431-0233; T-F, guided
tour every 40 minutes from 1–3:40; Sat/Sun every 30 minutes,
11–4:30; $7–10). These tours through the streets and recreated
apartments belonging to century-old immigrant life offer a
remarkable imaginative experience of old New York. Afterwards,
continue south to the **discount shops of Orchard Street** such as
Forman's (82 Orchard) and **Chock's** (74 Orchard), old standbys
among a plethora of newer entries.

Where Orchard St. intersects Grand St., turn right to complete your circle at the nearby subway. But if you want to treat
those tired tootsies to a **Chinese accupressure foot massage**,
continue west on Grand across 3rd Ave. (the Bowery) for just a
few blocks to 179 Grand (at Baxter; 40 minutes $28.00; open til
9PM). At 87 Baxter, just south of Canal, is our favorite
Vietnamese Restaurant **Nha Trang.**

(If you missed the last tour at the Tenement Museum, an
interesting alternative is the **Asian American Arts Center** [26
Bowery 3rd fl.;1-212-233-2154; M-F 12:30–6PM; Th til 7:30],

which offers unusual artistic perspectives on the Asian American community.)

Directions (Due to subway construction) the **Grand Street** subway stop is currently reached by the Shuttle, one stop downtown from the Broadway-Lafayette IND station. If you've walked west on Grand St. for a foot massage and then on to the Nha Trang restuaurant, the nearest subway stations are the Canal St. #6 or the V/N/R trains, all on Bway.

Want To Know More? Two classics about the Lower East Side: "How the Other Half Lives,"Jacob Riis (1902) and Henry Roth's "Call It Sleep" (1934). See also "The Spirit of the Ghetto," Hutchins Hopgood (1967), Meredith Tax's novel "Rivington Street," Mimi Sheraton's "The Bialy Eaters: The Story of a Bread and a Lost World" (2000) and the 1975 film "Hester Street." For the East Village, see "McSorley's Wonderful Saloon," Joseph Mitchel (1992) and, for the area's hippie heyday, the film "Trash" (1970).

WALKING MAP

1. ICP
2. Bryant Park
3. NY Public Library
4. St. Patrick's Cathedral
5. Rockerfeller Center
6. IBM (The Dahesh Museum)
7. Paley Park

Quiet Gems of Midtown Manhattan

The International Center of Photography, New York Public Library, Dahesh Museum of Fine Arts and St. Patrick's Cathedral

On this city walking day which crosses roiling Midtown, the sites brim with art and atmosphere that still the urban din and calm jangled nerves. First is **The International Center of Photography**, where pictures speak silently but passionately, making meaning without words. The route then traverses beautifully restored **Bryant Park** to take us into the **New York Public Library**. Since 1911, this Beaux Arts "temple" has welcomed those who pass the scrutiny of New York's favorite felines, **Patience and Fortitude**, the sculpted marble lionesses who guard the Fifth Ave. entrance. (They don't look good in hats but are elegantly wreathed during the holiday season.) **Scandinavia House** is our favorite suggestion for lunch. A few blocks uptown, political demonstrations in front of **St Patrick's Cathedral** may be raucous, but the sublime interior is almost silent. Turn up the volume by crossing Fifth Avenue to **Rockefeller Center.** A northeast stroll leads to IBM, the new home of the **Dahesh Museum**, a center for 19th and early 20th century European art. **"The past never looked so good"** is the fitting subtext here. This perfect day comes to a close with a respite at the side of a city waterfall: either the noisy indoor splasher in garish, gorgeous **Trump Tower** or the quieting cascade in pretty vest-pocket **Paley Park**.

Today's excursion begins at the **International Center of Photography** (1133 6th Ave./43rd; 1-212-857-0000; T-Sun 10-5; F free 5-8; Adm. $7-10). New York is a photographer's town; ICP is the only museum devoted exclusively to photography and to demonstrating its versatility as a medium: as an agent of social change, as fine art, as a means of research, as a venue for self-expression. You may catch their Trienniale, a panoramic survey of photography and electronic imaging from around the world.

Walk one block south to stroll through **Bryant Park** (W. 42nd St. bet. 6th Ave. and The New York Public Library), a formal garden park that is Midtown's only large green space. Established in 1871 and later redesigned through a competition among unemployed architects, it was recently restored. The park is named for the great abolitionist, poet, and editor, William Cullen Bryant (1794–1878) who wrote "Go forth under the open sky, and list to Nature's teachings." New Yorkers try to do that here during their lunch breaks **Hungry Now Or Later** If you are ready for a lunch break, there are several possibilities. The Library's outdoor **Terrace Café** (overlooking 5th Ave.) boasts "best sandwiches in New York City." They are good, as are the pastas and crepes. Tables fill up quickly at noon. Popular **Bryant Park Grill** (behind the Library), offers more serious dining. Find it near the sculpted bust of Gertrude Stein, one of the few public monuments to a woman in New York; only Eleanor Roosevelt, Golda Meir, and Alice in Wonderland have been so honored. For a Scandinavian treat, try **Aqcafe in Scandinavia House** (56 Park Ave./37th St); see interesting exhibits on the 3rd floor. Also, a few blocks downtown on 5th Ave. is the **Dining Commons of the Graduate School of the City University** (36th St.). Later in the day, find the snackbar under tall bamboo in the **IBM Atrium** (589 Madison Ave.), which houses the Dahesh Museum or relax at **Trump Tower café** (56th/5th Ave.).

After a break, the route continues in midpoint midtown at the **New York Public Library: Center for the Humanities** (42nd St./5th Ave.; 1-212-869-8089 (ask about Tours); T-Sat 11-6; cl. Sunday; free). Students grinding away on dissertations may not appreciate the beauty of the **recently restored reading rooms**, but visitors to the belle époque granddame—with its majestic columns and arches, gilded drinking fountains, grand marble staircases, and high painted ceilings—experience the best of Beaux Arts architecture. Pick up a floorplan in the stunning lobby where volunteers will help you determine a route based on your interests. **Changing exhibits** draw primarily upon the library's specialized collections. Take the elevator to the third floor rotunda to see **"The Story of the Recorded Word,"** four **fine WPA murals** and familiar portraits of famous Americans. A first draft of the **Declaration of Independence** in Thomas Jefferson's own hand, is sometimes displayed. The carefully underlined passages that advocate the abolition of slavery were later expurgated.

The route continues uptown to famed **St. Patrick's Cathedral** (51st St/5th Ave.). St. Patrick's (1878) is an adaptation of the French Gothic cathedral. Experience the graceful serene interior, particularly the stained glass windows and the Lady Chapel behind the altar. Twin 330 foot towers (1888) and the richly carved facade are a startling contrast to the **linear skyscrapers of Rockefeller Center** (47–52 Sts./between 5th and 6th Aves.).

A few blocks north is the **Dahesh Museum of Art** (580 Madison Ave./56th St.; 1-212-759-0606; T-Sat 11–6; free). Dahesh—"inspiring wonder"—is the adopted name of its founder, Lebanese philosopher Salim Moussa Achi (1909–1987), whose collection is the museum's foundation. **Most works illustrate stories from history, the bible, and mythology.** The style is realism enlivened with occasional over-the-top romantic flourishes. **Orientalism,** portrayals of the unfamiliar cultures of North Africa and the Middle East, is also well represented. These exotic, often erotic fantasies had particular appeal for the wealthy, repressed Victorian patrons who commissioned them.

In **Paley Park** (3 E. 53rd St.) today's last quiet gem, enjoy a snack near the 22 ft. high waterfall. The spray is cooling on summer days. Or, for glitz, return to 5th Ave. to the **Trump Tower Atrium.**

Directions The 6th Ave. line (F train) to 42nd St. for the ICP and NY Public Library. To return, Paley Park is close to the E/F and #6 stop at the 51st/Lexington Ave. station

Want To Know More See "Women as Portrayed in Orientalist Painting," Lynne Thornton (1994) and "Morgan: American Financier," a biography by Jean Strouse (1999). Websites: daheshmuseum.org, icp.org and scandinaviahouse.org.

On the Waterfront

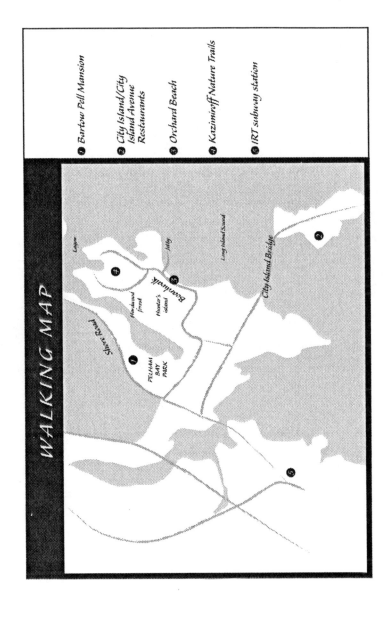

WALKING MAP

1. Bartow Pell Mansion
2. City Island/City Island Avenue Restaurants
3. Orchard Beach
4. Kazimiroff Nature Trails
5. IRT subway station

Wilderness and Waterfront
Pelham Bay Park and City Island

This great day in the upper Bronx offers a walk in **City Island,** a charming section of the Bronx with the air of a cozy New England village, **seafood restaurants** with city skyline views, a dip in the placid waters of Long Island Sound at **Orchard Beach,** and two short **nature trails** through shady forests and along rocky coastlines. We prefer the subway for this day, but if you're driving you may also have time for the **Pell-Bartow Mansion** in Pelham Bay Park.

Begin the day by taking the #6 (Pelham Bay-not Parkchester) local subway to the last stop, Pelham Park, a ride of under an hour. Downstairs, the Bx29 Bus goes directly to **City Island,** a 1.5 mile narrow spit of land on Long Island Sound, whose mile-long main street, City Island Avenue, is lined with clapboard houses, tiny antique shops, and spired churches. The island was settled by German and Scandanavian immigrants who developed a marine economy in the 19th century. Around 1900, City Island was home to many marine pilots, whose job was to board and guide steamships coming down from New England through the treacherous waters of Long Island Sound into Manhattan. In the first half of the 20th century, City Island was dominated by clamming, commercial fishing, lobstering, and shipbuilding. Now most City Islanders work off the island, and its marine past remains largely in its six yachting marinas, bait and tackle shops, marine-related businesses, and numerous seafood restaurants overlooking Long Island Sound and the New York City skyline.

Hungry? On City Island Avenue, near the bridge which connects the island to Pelham Bay Park, is the venerable **The Lobster Box** (34 City Island Ave.; 1-718 885-1952; 11:30–10 pm daily); at the end of City Island Avenue is the very casual Johnny's Famous **Reef Restaurant** (2 City Island Ave.; 1-718 885-2086, open all day), a favorite with locals and visitors for fried or steamed seafood plates. Johnny's 90 outdoor tables overlook Long Island Sound, the Throgs Neck and Whitestone Bridges, and in the distance, the city skyline. Other eateries popular with locals are the **Original Crab Shanty** (61 City Island Ave.; 1-800-640-6522; daily 11-midnight) or the legendary **Tito Puentes** (64 City Island Ave.; 1-718-855-3200, daily 11:30-midnight) with its murals of America's jazz greats.

After lunch, walk (or take the bus) back to the bridge and cross over into Pelham Bay Park. From the bridge it's only about a mile on a lovely, tree shaded walking path to Orchard Beach. **Orchard Beach** (lifeguards in season; changing rooms; fast food; parking all year $6), a cove on Long Island Sound, was built by Robert Moses in the 1930s, with sand trucked in from New Jersey and Queens. Its quiet waters are perfect for cooling off after a hot day. The **Kazimiroff Nature Trails,** two easy mile-long paths that loop through shady forests and along a rocky coastline, begin at the far (north) end of the beach. They are a good introduction to the oak-hickory forest and salty marshes of Pelham Bay Park, home to hawks, egrets, and warblers. From here you can catch the B12 bus back through Pelham Bay Park to the subway.

The short bus ride gives you a chance to reflect on a bit of New York history, in which Pelham Bay Park plays a role. In the 1600s, several English settlements were founded here by Puritan dissenters, among them Anne Hutchinson and John Throgmorton (for whom the Throg's Neck Bridge is named). When both settlements were wiped out in an Indian attack, the peninsula was abandoned. In 1776, during the American Revolution, the American Colonel John Glover held off an attempted amphibian landing on the peninsula by Britain's Hessian mercenaries. The

American troops, under the command of George Washington, made their escape north to White Plains and lived to fight another day (though they lost that battle as well). Seventy five years later, the area became the site of mansions of the well-to-do, of which only the Pell-Bartow mansion remains.

The **Bartow-Pell Mansion** (895 Shore Rd.; 1-718-885-1461; W/Sat/Sun 12–4; $2.50; www. bartowpellmansionmuseum.org), is several miles from Orchard Beach. There is no connecting bus between the two (or between the Mansion and City Island), but the Mansion can be reached by BX 45 bus from the Pelham Park subway station. The mansion is a modest Greek Revival home (circa 1840), whose authentic American Empire furnishings, lovely garden, and view of the Bay make it well worth a visit (across the road is the public golf course which has a nice veranda for eating lunch, rest rooms, and free parking).

Directions By subway: #6 Pelham Bay (not Parkchester) local to the last stop, Pelham Park. Under one hour from midtown Manhattan, half the ride is above ground with views of the Bronx. Downstairs, Bus Bx 29 goes to (and from) City Island via Orchard Beach. In the Summer busses from the subway run the 2.5 miles to the golf course, across the road from the Bartow-Pell Mansion. (Bikes are permitted on the subway, and on weekdays during the Spring and Summer this day can be done by bike. It's a pleasant 12 mile circular ride, which includes 2 miles of the Park's Greenbelt, just down the road from the Golf Course).

By car: take the FDR Drive to Bruckner Blvd; head toward I 95, New England Throughway, take Exit 8B, City Island/Orchard Beach, and follow the signs to City Island. Metered street parking on City Island Avenue (crowded on summer weekends); the restaurants have free parking. Orchard Beach Parking is $6; for the Pell Bartow Mansion, you can park free at the Golf Course.

Want To Know More? "The Beautiful Bronx, 1920–1950," Lloyd Ultan (1979); "The Last Algonquin," Theodore Kazimiroff, Jr. (2000); "Bronx Ecology: Blueprint for a New Environmentalism," Allen Hershkowitz (2002).

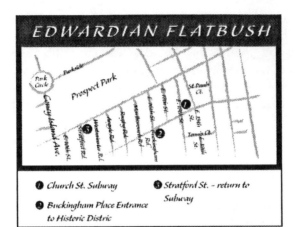

EDWARDIAN FLATBUSH

Prospect Park

Park Circle

Parkside

St. Paul's Ct.

Coney Island Ave.

Prospect Park

1 Church St. Subway

2 Buckingham Place Entrance to Historic Distric

3 Stratford St. – return to Subway

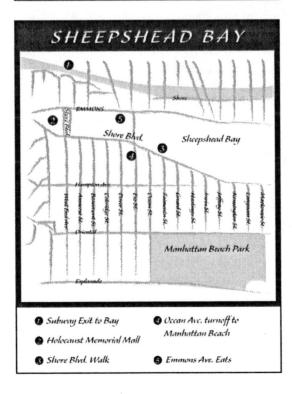

SHEEPSHEAD BAY

Shore

EMMONS

Shore Blvd.

Sheepshead Bay

Manhattan Beach Park

Esplanade

1 Subway Exit to Bay

2 Holocaust Memorial Mall

3 Shore Blvd. Walk

4 Ocean Ave. turnoff to Manhattan Beach

5 Emmons Ave. Eats

A Kinder, Gentler Brooklyn
Edwardian Flatbush and Sheepshead Bay

This beautiful Brooklyn day starts with a stroll through the leafy lanes and stunning architectural treasures of the **Prospect Park South Historic District**—not Buckingham Palace but **Buckingham Road, Albermarle Terrace,** and other gems of turn-of-the-century Flatbush. A short hop back on the subway takes you to **Sheepshead Bay** for lunch and a leisurely stroll along the channel of this former fishing village, which still retains its charming marine ambience (See Special Events, May). Nearby is the little-known but deeply affecting **Holocaust Memorial Mall,** with over 100 granite markers inscribed with brief texts, such as the description of Raoul Wallenberg's rescue of Hungarian Jews (Stone 133) and the biography of Emanual Ringelblum, a chronicler of the Warsaw Ghetto (Stone 145). In summer you can end this perfect day with a walk or swim at **Manhattan Beach**—a turn-of-the-century watering hole for Brooklyn's elite—which offers gentler surf and fewer people than nearby Brighton or Coney.

For the **Prospect Park South** walk, hop any Q train to the Church Avenue station (18th St. exit). Walk right 2 blocks on vibrant Church Ave., a Caribbean and African commercial center. Turn left at **Buckingham Road,** marked by 2 stone piers. This divided, tree lined boulevard of flamboyant palatial homes in every imaginable style from columned Georgian to Japanese temple was developed at the turn of the century, after the newly-built Brighton Line made the neighborhood accessible to the genteel Brooklyn beaches as well as Manhattan. Amble up Buckingham Road, turn right on **Albermarle Road** and thread your way up and down **Marleborough, Rugby** (101 is the house in the film "Sophie's Choice"), **Argyle, Westminister, and Stratford Roads,** back to the Church Ave. subway. (See Special Events, April for house tours of the area.)

Hop back on the Q train to **Sheepshead Bay** station (Sheepshead Bay/15th St. exit) and turn left down a few commercial blocks to Emmons Ave. on the channel. Turn left here for the **Holocaust Memorial Mall.** At the end of the park cross the footbridge onto **Shore Boulevard,** which offers a charming view of the bustling, boat-filled channel for about 1 mile. At this point you can decide whether to turn left at the walkway's end onto Emmons Ave. back to your starting point or continue on to Manhattan Beach.

For **Manhattan Beach,** make a right turn off Sheepshead Bay's Shore Blvd. at Ocean Ave., walk right 3 blocks to Oriental Blvd., turn left and continue just past Pat Parlato playground. At Falmouth St. turn right for 1 block to Manhattan Beach (picnic tables, snack bar and restrooms in season).

Hungry? Lunch options at Sheepshead Bay are grouped fairly close together on Emmons Ave. not far from the footbridge. One neighborhood standby is **Randazzo's** (2019 Emmons Ave.; 1-718-615-0010), a paragon of a clam bar that also serves up a great pasta with lobster sauce. **Lundy's,** the landmark fish restaurant (1901 Emmons; 1-718-743-0022) has been a draw for decades. **El Greco Diner,** for a lighter repast, is nearby on the corner of Emmons Ave.

Directions Any Q train goes to both the Church St. station for Edwardian Flatbush and to Sheepshead Bay station. For Manhattan Beach, turn off Sheepshead Bay's Shore Blvd. at Ocean Ave., walk right 3 blocks to Oriental Blvd., turn left and continue just past Pat Parlato playground. At Falmouth St. turn right for 1 block to Manhattan Beach.

Want To Know More? For architectural details about specific Prospect Park South homes see the AIA Guide; for April house tours call Flatbush Development Corporation, 1-718-469-5064. For Sheepshead Bay, see Brian Merlis, Lee A. Rosensweig and I. Stephen Miller, "Brooklyn's Gold Coast: The Sheepshead Bay Communities" (1997). For half day or evening boat trips, call Dorothy B, 1-718-646-4057 or Sea Queen IV 1-718-332-2423. For information on inscribing a Holocaust Memorial Mall stone, call Rosen Monuments, 1-718-961-6900.

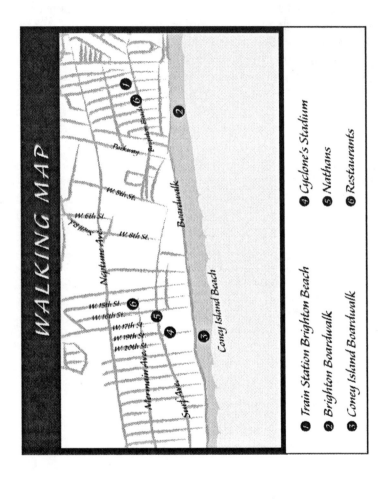

WALKING MAP

① Train Station Brighton Beach
② Brighton Boardwalk
③ Coney Island Boardwalk
④ Cyclone's Stadium
⑤ Nathans
⑥ Restaurants

Life's a Beach

A Great Day at Brighton and Coney Island

Can't afford a trip to Russia? No problem. Today's excursion takes you to Little Odessa, the newest transformation of **Brighton Beach**, as well as to the many attractions of **Coney Island**, including the **New York Aquarium**. And all for the price of a subway token! Authentic **Russian food** abounds (and some classic Italian as well), or you can opt for a traditional Nathan's hot dog. You might want to round out a summertime visit with a **Brooklyn Cyclones** baseball game in the evening; also in Summer is the Mermaid Parade, usually the last weekend in June. If you visit in Winter, choose the Polar Bear Club's annual immersion in the freezing surf in January (see Special Events).

The fun begins with the subway ride, as the Q train to **Brighton Beach** emerges over the Manhattan Bridge, giving fabulous views of lower Manhattan (check the trains; for the next two years the Manhattan Bridge is being renovated and all Brighton trains go underground). Exit at the Brighton Beach Ave. station, descend the stairs and turn left to Brighton 7 St. (ahead a couple of blocks on Brighton Beach Ave. is the sign for Mrs. Stahl's Knishes—baked not fried!—one of only two authentic knish places left in New York). On the Boardwalk, the views to the left are of Manhattan Beach and Breezy Point, called the Irish Riviera because so many police and fire people live there. To the right, the direction of your walk, you'll see the towering Coney Island parachute jump (alas, no longer in operation), with the New Jersey headlands in the far distance.

A lot has changed in **Brighton Beach** over the last century but the sea, sand, and sky are as bright as ever. A century ago Brighton Beach was a center of thoroughbred racing and an elegant beach resort. In 1907 the Brighton Beach Baths opened with swimming pools, tennis courts and entertainment. From the 1920s to the 1950s, six story apartment buildings housed a growing middle class Jewish, Irish, and German population moving out of the poorer sections of Brooklyn. After the 1960s, the area went into decline but now is again being transformed as the Baths have been demolished to make way for condos costing upward of half a million dollars. The immigration of thousands of Russian Jews to the area has led to the opening of many ethnic restaurants, nightclubs and specialty shops. (You many want to pick up a bottle of Russian wine such as Kungsmarauli, or Stalin's favorite, the fruity Bilvino Georgian Red Bahykapa.) As "Little Odessa," Brighton Beach is fast becoming one of the city's most exciting neighborhoods.

As you walk the boardwalk toward **Coney Island**, you'll pass a terrific children's playground (and a toilet facility, open 10-6) at Brighton 2nd St. The beach, boardwalk and fishing pier are filled with New Yorkers in all their diversity: hip hop teenagers, old guys playing handball in the adjacent courts, young parents pushing baby carriages, senior citizens sitting under the few shaded pavilions playing cards, NYC public school kids representing the city's racial and cultural rainbow on a visit to the Aquarium and joggers, walkers and treasure hunters. *Zoftig* Russian matrons in bikinis give the place the ambience of a Black Sea resort. At Surf Avenue and W. 8th St. you reach the **New York Aquarium** (1-718-265-3474; daily 10–6, all year; adm. $7–11), the first aquarium to breed and exhibit Beluga whales. (If you want to begin your day here, take the F train to the W. 8th St. Station.)

Coney Island really begins at W. 10th St. Named by the Dutch for the abundance of wild rabbits (konijn) here in the 17th century, Coney Island has undergone many changes. After the Civil War, development accelerated as railroads were built connecting the area to the rest of Brooklyn. In the 1870s and '80s, Coney Island became famous for the frankfurter and mixed public bathing, the carousel and the roller coaster, and infamous for its gambling dens, dancehalls and brothels. At the turn of the century, three amusement parks opened on the boardwalk (the most well known was Steeplechase, where Marilyn Monroe's skirt flew up from the air pumped from the underground grates). In 1910 Italian and Jewish immigrants began moving into Coney Island and, with the completion of the subway in 1920, the area attracted over a million people a day.

Between 1935 and the 1960s, when Robert Moses headed the City Parks Department, Coney Island changed again. Moses put restraints on commercial establishments (which he hated), opened Jones Beach, which drew the crowds further out on Long Island, and widened the Coney Island beach and boardwalk, effectively ousting the smaller mechanical rides adjacent to the beach. The abandoned entertainment areas gave way to public housing, and in 1964 Steeplechase Park and the parachute jump closed. But now some rides are back, the **Cyclone** and the **Ferris Wheel** ($5) are as thrilling as ever, and New Yorkers and tourists alike are rediscovering the joys of this quintessential New York playground.

Hungry? There's a wide range of choices. **Nathan's** has a small place on the boardwalk, but the original, opened in 1916, is on Surf Ave., two blocks off the boardwalk at Bay 16 St. Also just a few blocks off the Boardwalk are the well-known Italian restaurants **Carolina** (1409 Mermaid Ave./W 15th St.; 1-718-714-1294; daily noon-10) and **Gargiulo's** (2911 W.15th St., between Mermaid and Surf Ave., 1-718-266-4891; noon-10; cl. T [Both these restaurants have long waits on weekends and during the prime dinner hour]). For authentic Russian food, try **Dynasty** (309 Brighton Beach Ave. between Brighton Beach 3–4 Sts.; 1-718-891-2000, lunch, S-Th only; F/Sat, dinner until the wee hours). There are several Russian cafes on the boardwalk, better for a drink and the view, than the food.

Back on the boardwalk, continue walking towards Coney Island. Near the fishing pier, between 17–19th Sts., is the newest amusement, the Mets Minor League **Brooklyn Cyclones Keyspan Stadium** (schedule available at Tourist Information Booths around town or on the net, www.brooklyncyclones.com, or call 1-718-449-8497; tickets $5–10; starting times around 7 PM). These games have become a real Brooklyn institution: all the seats are good, there's kitchy entertainment between innings and a nice family crowd (you can't bring in your own food or drink; the usual high priced eats are available inside), and sometimes a free souvenir. If you don't expect the likes of Babe Ruth and Jackie Robinson, the setting and ambience makes this a very special evening anyway.

Past the stadium, at 21st St., is the colorful terra cotta and stucco building which used to house the Child's Restaurant, another old New York institution. It is now a neglected warehouse, but it may get a new life if it qualifies for historical landmark status. If you walk all the way to the end of the boardwalk, you hit Seagate, a gated community whose residents like to consider themselves separate from the adjacent neighborhoods. And if you're planning a trip to Brighton and Coney in June, check out the Mermaid Parade, usually the last weekend in June (see Special Events).

Directions Several 6th Ave. subway lines go to Brighton and Coney Island; check for the latest information due to extensive repair work; Q to Brighton Beach Ave., about 45 minutes; F to 8th St., Coney Island and the Aquarium (these run express or local on different days). To reverse the order of the day, board the N train to the last stop (Stillwell Ave./Coney Island) and then walk back to Brighton Beach for the train home.

By car: Parking is difficult but if you want to drive, take the Belt Parkway. There is metered parking at Brighton 7 St., Brighton 12 St. (adjacent to the playground, up to 5 hour limit depending on the season, $1 per hour) and at the Aquarium ($7).

Want To Know More? Neil Simon's film, "Brighton Beach Memoirs," takes place in the 1940s. Scott Haskins, "Sasha's Tricks" (2003); Woody Register, "The Kid of Coney Island: Fred Thompson and the Rise of the American Amusements" (2001); "Dreamland," Kevin Baker (1999); and "Coney Island: The People's Playground," by Michael Immerso offer interesting takes on Coney Island and Brighton Beach. An award winning video about the 60s generation in Brighton Beach is "The Boys of 2nd St. Park," by Dan Klores and Ron Berger.

HIKING MAP

HUDSON TERRACE

⑤

④

③

HUDSON RIVER

⑥

②

GEORGE WASHINGTON BRIDGE

①

RIVER RD.

---

❶ *Little Red Lighthouse,*
NYC Side

❷ *GWB Exit —— Palisades*
Longwalk Begins

❸ *Gas Station Snack Center*

❹ *Allison Park*

❺ *Dykman Hill descent to*
Hudson River

❻ *Boat Basin*

High on the Hudson

The George Washington Bridge and the Palisades Long and Shore Walk Loop

For thousands of New York City kids on their way to summer camps or family holidays in New Jersey, the spectacular span of the **George Washington Bridge** symbolized the entrance to "the country," where Nature reigned supreme. To a surprising extent, Nature still does. Traversing this "most beautiful bridge in the world," as the French architect Le Corbusier called it, is a thrilling experience and the start of a day away from the city's *angst*. The easy, under-5-mile loop on the **Long Walk and Shore Paths** takes the hiker along the top of the Palisade cliffs to Allison Park, where benches permit splendid viewpoints of Manhattan, and then down to the Hudson shore, where the view of the Palisades cliffs themselves are spectacular. (To regain the Bridge at the end of the Shore Path there is a long climb up a flight of stairs.) Bring binoculars, lunch and drink (restrooms and decent eats are available at the convenience store in the gas station complex about ¾ of the way through the Long Walk) and mosquito repellent in summer. Dress for the weather: it's windier on the bridge than down below, and carry single dollar bills and quarters in case you want to bus back to the city.

To access the **George Washington Bridge Pedestrian Walkway**, take the A train to the 175th St. station; enter into the Port Authority Bus Terminal and exit via Fort Washington Ave./178th St. to the street. Turn left for two blocks to

Pinehurst Ave. and Cabrini Blvd., where the terrain falls off steeply. Ahead is the huge soaring tower of the bridge and a Bike (pedestrian) Path sign for the bridge walkway. The bucolic views upriver seem little changed from 150 years ago. **Look behind you**, down to the left, for the **Little Red Lighthouse** (1-212-304-2365; accessed at 181st St. and Pinehurst Ave. via steps and an underpass), an 1880s structure made famous by the 1930s children story. Ahead are the uniquely columnar, vertically-striated Palisades, whose French explorers, visualizing them as encircling stockade posts, derived the name from the French verb *paliser,* "to enclose." Halfway through the Bridge walk you can enjoy equidistant views of the Palisades basalt cliffs on the Jersey side mirroring the manmade skyscraper "cliffs" of Manhattan. The Palisades, which the Native Americans called "rocks that look like trees," were formed 200 million years ago when underground molten rock called magma was compressed below the earth's surface and cooled in a peculiar process that allowed dark pyroxene and lighter feldspar crystals to develop into the coarse-grained striations that characterize these cliffs.

The **Bridge** itself, completed in 1931, is a miracle of engineering and an aesthetic delight, its towers a web of squares and triangles like erector set constructions created by giants. The delicate braided steel suspender ropes that loop over the cables above the roadway seem to magically hold the road up above the lower level, which was added in 1962. A 90x60 foot American flag housed inside the New Jersey tower is flown on patriotic occasions; before its special boom was built, it took 13 men to raise the flag and on a windy day, gusts would sometimes lift the men right off the deck.

To begin the **Palisades Long Walk**, turn right at the end of the Bridge's pedestrian walkway, cross at the Stop sign to the corner, and mount the iron staircase on your right (despite continuing construction work, entrance is permitted). Follow the mesh bridge to the trail, marked with green tree patches, straight ahead of you. The path wanders through the trees with the Palisades cliffs about 100 feet to your right (a roadway intermittently comes into view on your left). Several easily recognisable cut-off paths lead a few feet to splendid river overlooks. In Winter, you may see (and smell) wonderfully fragrant wild roses. After the large gas station complex visible on your left, continue on the trail a short way to a green iron fence. Follow the fence around to the entrance of Allison Park, a lovely resting spot facing the river. You can head back the way you came in, but....

To continue the **Loop Shore Path**, exit Allison Park by its further gate and turn right on the paved road for about ¼ mile until you see St. Joseph's College. Just past the College, look left for the small, rather obscured New York State Trail sign. Follow this sign for about ½ mile to the Dykman Hill intersection, hike down the hill for a right turn to the Boat Basin and continue your hike to the long flight of stairs up to the Bridge again.

Directions To the Bridge: IND A train to 175th St. station, Port Authority Bus Terminal; follow directions to access as above. To return to Manhattan by bus, walk 1 block left of the Bridge walkway to the traffic light, turn up the hill, staying on your right. At the top of the hill, cross Martha Washington Ave. turn right (by a huge auto sales lot), and continue to the corner. Turn left around the corner for the bus stop (busses pass every 15–20 minutes).

Want To Know More? Website: www.njpalisades.org. John Serrao, "The Wild Palisades of the Hudson" (1986); Robert O. Binnewies, "Palisades: 100,000 Acres in 100 Years" (2001). "The Little Red Lighthouse and the Great Gray Bridge" by Hildegarde Swift is reprinted in a modern edition.

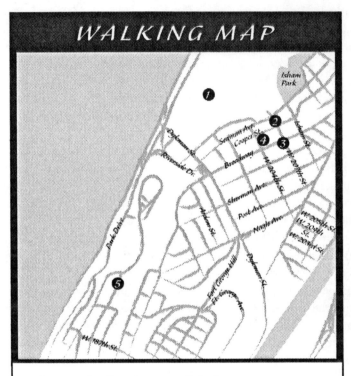

WALKING MAP

1. Inwood Hill Park
2. Restaurants
3. A Train Station
4. Dykman House
5. The Cloisters

Nature, Art and History at the Northern Tip of Manhattan
Inwood Hill Park and the Cloisters Museum

An easy, direct subway ride to upper Manhattan takes you on this perfect day to **Inwood Hill Park** (Broadway and 215th St.)—the only remnant of natural forest in Manhattan, **great Latino food** in the surrounding Mexican and Dominican neighborhood and then to the marvelous **Cloisters Museum**, the medieval art collection of the Metropolitan Museum, located in Fort Tryon Park.

Inwood was once a fertile hunting ground for Weckquasgeek Indians and the place where Peter Minuit bought the island of Manhattan for the equivalent of $24. The area was settled by the Dutch in the 18th century and was the site of a major Revolutionary War fight, the Battle of Harlem Heights. **Inwood Hill Park** at the northwestern tip of Manhattan is a 197 acre rocky expanse of oak, tulip, maple, hickory and dogwood trees with six miles of hiking trails, a salt marsh and one of Manhattan's last rural legacies, the colonial Dyckman House, now a farmhouse museum (4881 Bway at 204th St.; 1-212-304-9422, variable hours [temporarily closed for renovation]).

Once you're on the hiking trails in the park, the dense woods and diverse bird population impart the feeling of a true wilderness far from the city. Designed by the architect of Central Park, Frederick Law Olmsted, Inwood Hill Park features spectacular views of the Palisades, Indian caves, and ancient Indian burial sites in nearby Isham Park. Enthusiastic, knowledgeable Forest Rangers lead many interesting historical and nature trips within the park—even by canoe—and through the surrounding neighborhood. Pick up maps of the park and a tour schedule from the **Urban Ecology Center** (inside the park at 218th St. and Indian Rd., 1-888-697-2757 or 1-800-201-PARK; open all year 11-4 weekdays; 9–4 weekends). The most dramatic of the park's entrances is from the north, along 218th St., a five-minute walk from the 215th subway station on the IRT Broadway #1/9 local train. At 200 18th St. turn west (left) a few blocks through a quiet residential neighborhood.

Hungry? After your hike, try one of the many ethnic restaurants on 207th St., the neighborhood's main thoroughfare. Inwood has an ethnically diverse history. In the 1930s, working-class Irish and Germans settled there in the low rise apartment houses—there were even farms there then—but by the 1960s, the farms had disappeared and Puerto Rican and Cuban families moved in. More recently, Inwood has seen the immigration of Mexicans and Dominicans, more of whom live here than in any other place in the United States. This ethnic diversity can be sampled in the many good restaurants that line 207th St. and surrounding blocks. Tasty seafood is the specialty at **Mi Pequena Espana** (606 207th St.; 1-800-535-6016). One of our favorite Mexican restaurants is **Hopping' Jalapenos** (597 W. 207th; 1-212-569-6059, daily M-F, S/Sun brunch; huge portions). **The Piper's Kilt** (4944 Broadway, at 207th St., 1-212-569-7071) is a popular Irish brunch spot recalling an earlier immigration.

You can work off your delicious lunch by walking the mile or so down Broadway to the next stop, **The Cloisters Museum** in **Fort Tryon Park** (193rd St. and Fort Washington Ave.; 1-212-923-3700; T-Sun 9:30–5; closed major holidays; suggested adm.). Or take the A train, on the corner of 207th and Broadway to 190th St. The Cloisters, devoted to the architecture and art of Medieval Europe, permanently exhibits extraordinary medieval sculpture, the famed **Unicorn Tapestries**, and other visual splendors such as illuminated manuscripts, stained glass and decorative arts in all the precious metals. Its flower and herb gardens contain a diversity of medieval plants. Adjacent to the Cloisters is the glorious **Heather Garden**, won after a tough political fight by Washington Heights residents. Its setting in Fort Tryon Park overlooking the Hudson is fantastic in all seasons, and Winter snows add a particular beauty to the views. In the Summer you can enjoy a coffee and snack in the Cloisters Café.

Directions #1/9 local to 215th St. (about ½ hour). To the Cloisters, the A train on 207th and Broadway to 190th St. stop.

Want To Know More? Thomas Kelly, "The Rackets" (fiction; 2001); Augustin Lao-Montes and Arlene Davila, "The Latinization of New York City" (2001). The Dominican film "Red Passport/Passaporte rojo (2003) offers an authentic look at the Washington Heights neighborhood.

WALKING MAP

E 86th St
E 85th St
E 84th St
E 83rd St
E 82nd St
E 81st St
E 80th St

3rd Ave
2nd Ave
1st Ave
York Ave
East End Ave

E 79th St

E 78th St
E 77th St
E 76th St

Cherokee Pl

E 75th St
E 74nd St
E 73rd St
E 72nd St

Park Ave

❶

❺

E 71st St
E 70th St
E 69th St
E 68th St

②A

E 67th St

E 66th St
E 65th St
E 64th St
E 63rd St
E 62nd St
E 61st St
E 60th St

❸

❹

Queensboro Bridge

E 59th St

②B

Madison Ave

E 58th St

②C

Park Ave

E 57th St
E 56th St
E 55th St
E 54th St
E 53rd St
E 52nd St

❶ Sotheby's Auction House

❺ Mt. Vernon Hotel Museum

②A – ②C Good Eats

❹ Roosevelt Island Tram

❺ Roosevelt Island
    Waterside Path

Isles of Joy
Manhattan's Silk Stocking District and Roosevelt Island

Manhattan's "silk stocking" district, or Upper East Side, was once the sleepy village of Bloomingdale on the banks of the East River. In the 1830s, day trippers from lower Manhattan spent *their* "perfect days" here at the charming **Mount Vernon Hotel**, whose riverside lounges offered views of "gay sailing craft [and] a little spirits and water, or lemonade." Now a **Museum**, this charming house and garden will transport you back to this elegant era. In the 1860s, the infamous Boss Tweed developed the land between 68th and 69th Sts. and 4th and Madison Aves. into "one of the [city's] most desirable and picturesque localities for residence." Carriageways and paved streets, brilliantly lit by fancy streetlights, were frequented by silk stockinged ladies and their companions enjoying an upscale lifestyle. Today, the legendary **Sotheby's Auction House** lets you peek at—and bid on—some of the treasures of that period. But, visible to the elite was an island in the middle of the East River that none would wish to visit back then. **Roosevelt Island** (then called Welfare Island), though seemingly bucolic, seethed with the inmates of city institutions so inhuman that they shocked Charles Dickens. Now, however, whisked to the Island by its **spectacular Tram**, the stroller enjoys the tranquility of a leafy suburb and an awesome view of Manhattan's gilded towers shimmering in the refracted light of the river.

Begin with a morning auction at **Sotheby's Auction House** (1334 York Ave. at 71st St.; 1-212-606-7000; call for current exhibition and auctions, usually daily, M-Sat 10:15AM and 2:15PM [lasting for about 2 hours, enter any time]; exhibitions only on Sun 1–5). Exit the #6 train at the 68th St. station and walk east (try 69th St. for characteristic "silk stocking" blocks) to York Ave. Auctioneering takes place on the 7th floor. A catalogue ($4 at the reception desk) enhances your understanding of the fascinating antique furniture, jewelry and other quality items from America's past, but it's fun just to take a seat and watch the auction process. Don't dare scratch your nose or you may wind up with a $1000 Victorian mourning picture! Exhibitions of the next week's items are on the 10th floor, enhanced by witty period settings. A pleasant terraced cafe offers coffee, wine and light snacks.

Hungry? Ready for lunch before your Hotel Museum visit? One of our favorites is the tiny, inexpensive Lebanese restaurant **Maryum's Kitchen** (411 E. 70th; 1-212-744-3115). For the 10 blocks down to the Hotel Museum, all along 1st and 2nd Ave., there are upscale restaurants, cozy cafes and informal eateries, many with outdoor seating.

The short walk downtown (or the 2nd Ave. bus) quickly brings you to the **Mount Vernon Hotel Museum and Garden**, originally the site of the Abigail Adams carriage house (421 E. 61st St.; 1-212-838-6878; $5; T-Sun 11AM-4PM; cl. Aug; docent tours hourly). Visitors are given the same warm welcome as the Hotel offered "fashionable "persons taking their evening ride or drive from New York," over 170 years ago, when the city ended at 14th St.

Hungry Now? After your Hotel Museum visit, walk a few blocks down to E. 58th St., where the stretch between 2nd and 3rd Aves. offers some excellent choices such as the two-decades old **Felidia** (243 E. 58th St.) with its beautiful etched glass window and perfect pastas; **Chola** (232 E. 58th St.), whose upscale Mughal Indian lunch buffet gets top ratings, or **The Townhouse** (206 E.

58th St., closer to 3rd Ave.) offering a $10 express lunch in a quiet, silk-stocking setting. (Or you may want to have dinner in this area after your Roosevelt Island visit.)

Your afternoon destination is the **Roosevelt Island Tram** on 60th St. and 1st Ave. (every 15 minutes 6AM-2:30AM; $1.50 in **coins only**) for a spectacular 5 minutes aboard America's only commuter aerial ride. Today, **Roosevelt Island** (named after FDR) is home to a successful 1970s experiment in multi-income, multi-ethnic urban living. European habitation of the island began in the 1600s, when the Dutch bought it from the Indians for pig pasturing; hence its first name, "Hog Island." Named "Welfare Island" in 1828, it became "home" to a city-built workhouse, madhouse, almshouse and prison. Ironically, Boss Tweed, responsible for the grand vision of the "silk stocking" district directly across the river, was later an inmate on the Island, albeit a privileged one with his own vegetable garden, silk bathrobes and female visitors.

For the under-2-mile **Waterside path** around Roosevelt Island, turn right from the Tram. Sparkling views of Manhattan on one side and the remains of the 19th century Smallpox and Charity Hospitals, built of granite quarried on the island by convicts, meet your eyes. Don't miss Tom Otterness' charming sculpture group "The Marriage of Money and Real Estate" (1996) in the river itself. At the North Point Stone Lighthouse, the path turns towards the Queens side. Here the river narrows into an industrial riverscape out of a 1930s Charles Schiele painting: barges and tugs; the working sculpture garden of Socrates Park; the Adirondack Furniture factory, which made the glider planes for the Normandy invasion and still makes the famous Adirondack lounge chair; and the candy striped smokestacks of Con Ed's generator "Big Allis" towering over all. At the communal garden, turn right for your return, past the old Blackwell House, back to the Tram.

Directions Lexington Avenue #6 subway to 68th Street station; walk east and north to York Ave./71st for Sotheby's. The

Tram ($1.50 **coins only**) at 60th St. and 1st Ave. is accessed by the #4/5/6 trains or the N/R at the 59th Street station.

Want To Know More? For the "silk stocking" district: Louis Auchinloss, "Portrait in Brownstone" (1962); Casper Citron, "John V. Lindsay and the Silk Stocking Story" (1985). The film "Nighthawks" (1981) includes Tram action. Roosevelt Island information appears in "The Other Islands of New York City: A History and Guide," Sharon Seitz and Stuart Miller (2001). Linda Fairstein's "The Deadhouse" (2001) is a *policier* with a Roosevelt Island setting.

BIKING MAP

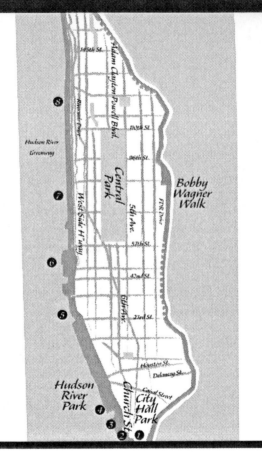

145th St.

Adam Clayton Powell Blvd.

Riverside Drive

110th St.

Hudson River Greenway

96th St.

Central Park

5th Ave.

FDR Drive

Bobby Wagner Walk

West Side H'way

57th St.

42nd St.

6th Ave.

23rd St.

Houston St.

Delancey St.

Canal Street

Hudson River Park

Church St.

City Hall Park

❶ Battery Park

❷ Holocaust Museum

❸ Otterness Sculptures

❹ Downtown Boathouse

❺ Chelsea Piers

❻ The Intrepid

❼ 79th St. Cafe

❽ Cherry Walk

Big Wheels, Little Wheels
Rolling on the Hudson River Bikeway

One of the most exciting ways to spend a day in New York City is rolling on your bike along **the Hudson River Bikeway**, which runs in a continuous off-road route for about 7 miles, north from Battery Park to 125th St. If the current Mayor sticks to his promises, this pedestrian and bike path will eventually circle the entire island of Manhattan (walkers can do various portions of the walk on separate days). If you don't have your own bike, in the Summer you can rent bikes at the booths in several places along the river: Battery Park, Chelsea Piers and near the Intrepid Museum at 44th St. (River Bikes: 64 North River; 1-212-967-5444, May–Oct).

This great biking day starts at Battery Park, the southern end of the route, because going south to north gives you the best Hudson River views. There are plenty of diversions and places to eat along the way, so be sure to **bring your bike lock**. In addition to the views and unique landscaping and flower gardens, you'll also see the diversity of New York's residents—walking, riding, roller blading, sunning on the lawns, schmoozing, and enjoying their own city.

Because the bike path became so popular, it is separated from the pedestrian walkway (at this time you can still ride adjacent to the river up to Chambers St., but that may change). Soon after you begin the ride, you pass the Museum of Jewish Heritage-A Living Memorial to the Holocaust (18 First Pl., Battery Park City; 1-212-509-6130; Sun-W 10–5:45 and some evenings; $7 adm.), which now has a rooftop memorial garden and kosher cafeteria [museum admission not required]). You then pass the World Financial Center, reconstructed to its original beauty after its damage on 9/11. Here there's a turn to the right: just before reaching Stuyvesant High School, where the bikeway again turns north, make a right into the small park just behind the school, to see the wonderfully inventive and whimsical **bronze sculptures of Tom Otterness**. Continue north, along the River past Stuyvesant High School, one of the best public high schools in the country and the home of many Westinghouse Science winners. Pier 25 has activities for children, including a miniature golf range, and then at Pier 26, the Downtown Boathouse (also at 79th St. Boat Basin; May to Oct; 1-646-613-0375) offers free kayaking evenings and weekends. In another mile or so, you'll reach the Greenwich Village access to the bikeway (public parking on Pier 40). As you continue up to 14th St., note the gentrification in the form of small, renovated apartment buildings on your right.

At 14th St., you can detour for lunch at the cozy **Petit Abeille**, a Belgian restaurant at 14th St. and 9th Ave. known for its mussels and Belgian fries. This area was the old meat market and is now becoming an upscale area of boutiques and art galleries. (Also nearby, at 9th Ave. and 15th St., is the **Chelsea Market** for yummy sweets and fresh foods to take out or eat there.) Continuing north you reach the **Chelsea Piers** at 23rd St., an area of physical activities including basketball courts and an ice rink (the fate of the Piers is uncertain, all or part of it may be moved once the Hudson River Park is completed). If you want a coffee break here, try **Ruthy's Café** outdoors behind the Piers, (they also have a bakery in the Chelsea Market) with its scrumptious cakes and pastries.

At 44th St. is the outdoor **Intrepid Sea Air Space Museum** (Pier 86, 46th St./12th Ave.; 1-212-245-0072; hours vary by season, daily 10–5, later in Summer; adm. $9-14), with its military and aircraft exhibits that are of special interest to history buffs (obey the lights around here, as there is an increase in vehicle traffic, since the docks that once berthed the likes of the Queen Mary and Ile de France are again in heavy use from cruise ships).

At 66th St. is a rusting hulk that may be kept as a work of public art. Just past it is the wonderful new pier at 70th St. that stretches way out into the water with gorgeous Hudson views in both directions. This is a good place to eat your lunch if you've brought it along. At 79th St. (restrooms available) is the 79th St. Boat Basin, where some folks actually live on their boats. There's also the new Boat Basin Café, a great place for a casual (and very reasonable) lunch.

At 91st St. you'll have to detour away from the water, under the roadway and up a hill, but the beautiful Riverside garden at the top makes it a rewarding diversion. At the end of the garden, down the hill, you're back on the bikeway for one of its most beautiful sectors, **Cherry Walk**, which takes you along the river all the way up to 125th St. As the path is not completed beyond this point, turn around here for the ride back downtown.

If you want to lengthen your ride, when you return to the starting point at Battery Park you can continue to ride up along the East River (for a short bit past the Staten Island Ferry you'll have to walk your bike) for some more gorgeous views of New York's east side skyline. You'll pass the **South Street Seaport**, with its restaurants, ship museums and shops. (If you do this on a weekday, you will have to walk your bike for a bit past the busy Fulton Fish Market, which is closed on weekends.) Past the Seaport, the East River Park (see Grand Street Circle) has interesting historic signs, and at 34th St. is the elegant Waterside Restaurant, which has a great weekend brunch. The off-road bike path now continues up to 42nd St.

This day is a great way to see New York City—so get out there and RIDE!

Want To Know More? For more biking routes and directions in the city, see http://www.transalt.org. For more on the Hudson River see "The Hudson River in Literature: an Anthology," Arthur Adams, ed. (1997) and "The Hudson: an Illustrated Guide to the Living River," Stephen Stanne et.al.(1996).

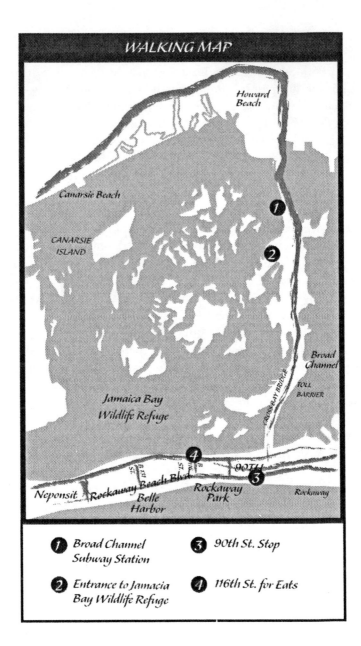

WALKING MAP

Howard Beach

Canarsie Beach

CANARSIE ISLAND

Broad Channel

TOLL BARRIER

RUSSBAY BRIDGE

Jamaica Bay Wildlife Refuge

B 115 ST.

B 116 ST.

90TH

Neponsit   Rockaway Beach Blvd.   Rockaway Park   Rockaway

Belle Harbor

1 Broad Channel Subway Station

3 90th St. Stop

2 Entrance to Jamacia Bay Wildlife Refuge

4 116th St. for Eats

Free as a Bird

Jamaica Bay Wildlife Refuge and Rockaway Beach Walk

Robert Moses did some nasty things to New York, but helping
to create the **Jamaica Bay Wildlife Refuge** wasn't one of them.
This urban refuge encompasses more than 9000 acres of diverse
habitats: salt marsh, fields, woods, various kinds of ponds and
an open expanse of Jamaica Bay. Winter, Spring, Summer and
Fall—all the seasons have a special appeal. May-September are
the best birding months, but even during late Fall or Winter you
may see "real birds" such as the yellow-rumped warbler, snow
goose or red-breasted Merganser. Off-season, both the Refuge
and the **Rockaway Beach Park Boardwalk** (biking ok except
Summer) offer a mood of tranquility. In Summer, you can end
with a swim at Rockaway Beach. You'll want to take these great
escapes more than once.

The **Jamaica Bay Wildlife Refuge** (1-718-318-4340) trails
are open daily sunrise-sunset (free parking, 8:30–5 except major
holidays; snacks only at the Visitors Center; restrooms; no food,
drink or smoking on the trail; bring a hat and binoculars; wear
long pants against poison ivy and ticks Mar-Sept; use mosquito
repellent in Summer). To reach the **Refuge**, take the A train
(towards Brooklyn) to the Broad Channel station. The ½ mile
walk to the Refuge (2 blocks west to Crossbay Boulevard; turn
right) takes you through the settlement of **Broad Channel**, a
19th century fishing village that still retains its marine ambience

in wood frame houses set over the water and boardwalks connecting one to another. These days, this tight community is populated largely by members of the uniformed services. The Refuge entrance/parking lot on your left is marked by a National Park Service sign. At the **Visitors Center**, pick up trail maps and informational pamphlets about the flowers, butterflies, birds and other creatures of the area, and the "**Trail Guide to the West Pond**" with its description of the flora and fauna at 13 stops (with benches) on the 1.25 mile trail. Look for the sign on your left that indicates the terrapin birthing grounds on the beach. Enjoy the views, spot the birds, and visit the South and North Garden diversions. Across from the Visitors Center is the mile-long trail around the East Pond, a haven for shore birds.

From the Bay to the Beach is a natural. **Rockaway** is a narrow spit of land, a barrier beach across Jamaica Bay. Originally settled in the mid-1660s by the British, it was only in the mid-1800s that a Canarsie ferry made the Rockaways accessible to wealthy summer visitors. Railway accessibility by the 1870s led to the development of elite resort hotels and a residential community on the water. The turn of the century saw the mass development of the Rockaways: the bay was partially filled in; a large boulevard and boardwalk were constructed; streets were laid out and an amusement park was built. By the 1940s, subway accessibility and mass car ownership made the area popular with day-trippers and working class Irish vacationers.

Refuge visitors have two public transportation options for continuing to **Rockaway Beach Park**. (For **bikers**, the Rockaway Beach Park Boardwalk can be accessed along the same route as the bus, or entirely by subway; then bikers can extend their day on the Boardwalk down to 9th St. or past 116th St.) A return to the Broad Channel train station for the Rockaway (NOT Far Rockaway) A or S train to **Rockaway Beach 90th St. station**, or, across the road from the Refuge entrance, the Q53 or Q21 bus (approximately every ½ hour, more frequently in summer) to **Rockaway Beach 90th St**. Both the subway and bus drop you off on Rockaway Beach Blvd.; the ocean is just a few blocks away. (Surfing legally takes place 3 streets lower down at Beach 87th St. if you want to take a look.) The **Rockaway Beach Park Boardwalk to Beach 116th St.** is a stretch kept clean and safe under the supervision of the National Park Service. **Note: swim only in life-guarded areas as high surfs and fast currents are common.**

Hungry? A BYO lunch at one of the Refuge's few picnic tables or, if it's Summer, a bite at a Rockaway Boardwalk snack bar are possible. However, if you can hold off until you arrive at **Rockaway Beach Blvd. and 116th St.** the small Salvadoran restaurant **Las Gemellas** (114-11 Rockaway Beach Blvd. at 116th St.; 1-718-634-5097) is recommended for its *pupusa,* stuffed pancakes, and inexpensive, hearty meals. Bob's on the Bay, at 116 St./Beach Channel, behind the Sunoco Gas station and Bob's Auto Repair yard offers "pub" food and glorious bay views.

Directions To the Refuge, the IND A train to Broad Channel Station; walk west to Cross Bay Blvd., then right for about ½ mile. To continue to the Rockaway beaches, either return to the Broad Channel station and take the Rockaway (NOT Far Rockaway) train or take the Q53 or Q21 busses opposite the Refuge on Cross Bay Boulevard. Your destination is Beach 90th St. in both cases; it's a few blocks to the beach. Return via the A train at Beach 116th St. and Rockaway Beach Blvd.

By car: take the Belt Parkway east to exit 17 (Cross Bay Blvd.), go over the North Channel Bridge and continue 1.5 miles to the Refuge. After leaving the Refuge, turn left (away from Broad Channel) to continue to Rockaway Beach 90th St.

Want To Know More? Browse the Refuge Bookshop; the website is www.nps.gov/gate. A Program and Activity Information guide, GATEWAY, is available at the Visitors Center. See John Bull, "Birds of the New York Area" (1964). The Brooklyn Bird Club website is www.brooklynbirdclub.org/jamaica.htm

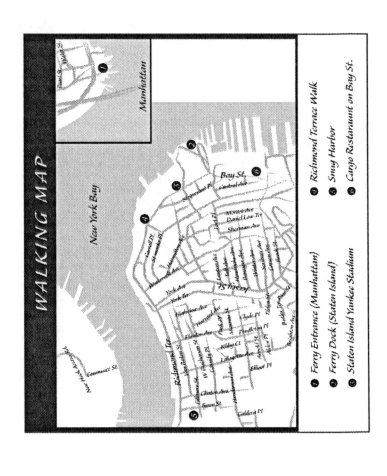

WALKING MAP

Manhattan

New York Bay

New York Harbor... Commerce St.

Bay St.
Central Ave.

Montroe Ave.
Daniel Low Tre
Sherman Ave

TS Ferry

Richmond Tre

❶ Ferry Entrance (Manhattan)   ❹ Richmond Terrace Walk
❷ Ferry Dock (Staten Island)   ❺ Smug Harbor
❸ Staten Island Yankee Stadium   ❻ Cargo Restaurant on Bay St.

Classic Staten Island

*The Ferry Crossing, Richmond Terrace
Walk to Snug Harbor Cultural Center, and
Baseball with a View*

From its first European settlement around 1630 until the building of the Verrazano Bridge in 1964, Staten Island, New York's "fifth borough," was accessible only by ferry. This classic Staten Island excursion begins with the **spectacular views from the free Staten Island Ferry**, rivalling those of any city in the world. Upon docking at St. George 25 minutes later, you begin an easy 2-mile waterfront walk from **Richmond Terrace to the Snug Harbor Cultural Center**, whose lovely gardens and grounds include the only **Chinese Scholar's Garden** in the United States (there's a **restaurant in the Garden** as well as a charming **cafe** outside, or you can BYO lunch). In season, the picture postcard view of Manhattan's night skyline from the family-friendly **Staten Island Yankees Stadium** (1-718-720-9265 or 876-6917; www.siyanks.com) on the river is a sports experience you'll never forget.

Nowhere is New York City's involvement with the sea clearer than on the **Staten Island Ferry crossing**. Available 24/7, 365 days a year, every ½ hour (every hour after midnight), the 300 year old Staten Island Ferry leaving Manhattan offers a breath-taking view aft, right, of the city's west side skyline, with the Empire State Building in the distance filling in the space left by the destroyed World Trade Center. Aft, left, Ellis Island and the

Statue of Liberty hove into view. On the return trip, the Brooklyn view offers 3 graceful suspension bridges: the Brooklyn, the Manhattan, and the Verrazano.

After exiting the Staten Island's Ferry Terminal, turn right for the waterfront's **Richmond Terrace walk to Snug Harbor.** (You can pick up your tickets for a **Staten Island Yankees game** at the Stadium just adjacent to the Ferry Terminal.) The pleasant stroll offers more gorgeous views of Manhattan's skyline. As you pass Kill van Kull, with its looming oil tanks, try to imagine this as 19th century New York's "country in the city," a place of fine resorts and a fairgrounds that boasted Barnum and Bailey circuses, Wild Bill Cody's frontier shows, and the home diamond of the city's earliest baseball team, the Metropolitans. After about 1.5 miles, at Jersey St., the Terrace ends and you rise up to street level for about another half mile to the gates of Snug Harbor Cultural Center.

Once a retirement home for seamen, the extensive grounds and gardens of **Snug Harbor** (1000 Richmond Terrace; 1-718-448-2500; grounds free) includes the Newhouse Center for Contemporary Art (W-Sun 11–5, $2); the Staten Island Botanic Garden (1-718-273-8200) and the wonderful **Chinese Scholar's Garden** (T-Sun 10–5 $5; call for special events around Chinese New Year). The Chinese Scholar's Garden offers moon gates, stone bridges, and all the other graceful and serene accoutrements of a typical Ming dynasty retreat. Other parts of the grounds include ponds, scenic walks, and a cafe.

A spectacular feature of a Staten Island day is the **return ferry trip at night,** so either take in that baseball game with a view or enjoy the remainder of your evening at the **Cargo Restaurant** (120 Bay St.; 1-718-876-0539; open daily, noon-2AM), which offers a full menu in a casual setting with live midweek jazz at 8PM (call to confirm). Bay St. is a tiny enclave 2 blocks left of the Ferry Terminal that forms part of an old, once important working lighthouse complex restoration.

Directions For the Staten Island Ferry take the #4/5 subway to Bowling Green; #1 subway to South Ferry or N train to Whitehall St.; then Staten Island Ferry (every ½ hour). Bus S40 from Ferry Terminal runs to and from Snug Harbor's front gate and the Yankees' Stadium.

Want to Know More? Bruce Kershner, "Secret Places of Staten Island" (1998); Charles I. Sachs, "Made on Staten Island: Agriculture, Industry and Suburban Living in New York" (1988).

Great Escapes

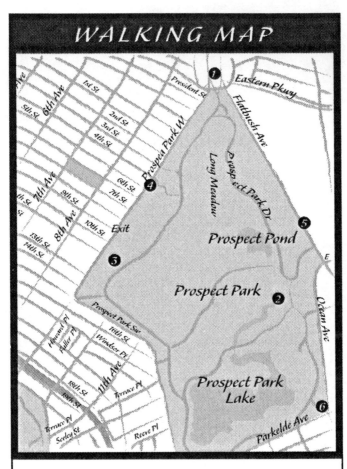

WALKING MAP

❶ Grand Army Plaza   ❺ Wildlife Center

❷ Boat House Visitor's Center   ❻ Drummer's Grove

❸ Bandshell

❹ Litchfield Villa

Under Blue Skies in Chocolate City

Prospect Park and Park Slope

So many brownstones lined the streets of New York in 1900 that a contemporary guidebook was titled "Chocolate City." Today, Brooklyn's village-like enclave, **Park Slope,** retains the same earthen-hued appearance of that time and place. In recent generations, the "Slope's" vitality has attracted numerous "brownstoners" intent on preserving and restoring stately townhouse-mansions and petite uniform row houses that charm strollers with their distinguishing ornamentation. Commercial avenues with no chain stores but plenty of independent small shops, bookstores, cafes and restaurants add to the flavor of old New York. On **Park Slope's** western border, **Prospect Park** (1866–1873) is the city's first royal green space made for unrestrained outdoor fun. Landscape architects Frederick Law Olmsted and Calvert Vaux designed the park to conform to the natural contours of the landscape. They preferred it to Central Park, their earlier, more languorous pastoral masterpiece. Green-wood Cemetery, also a historic predecessor, had a different primary function. (See Green-Wood Cemetery-Bay Ridge Day.) Prospect Park's 526 acres encompass a wildlife habitat, a bird sanctuary, and a cageless zoo. There are playing fields, cycling, hiking, and running paths, a real lake for boating and an artificial lake for skating. Architectural sites include the beautifully restored **Beaux Arts Boathouse,** Italianate Litchfield Villa and **Lefferts Homestead**—Brooklyn's oldest standing house. There are no skyscrapers on the endless encircling horizon, just, as above Park Slope, the usually blue and beautiful Brooklyn sky.

The #2/3 train stops at the Grand Army Plaza entrance to Prospect Park in Brooklyn; exit SW. The **Grand Army Plaza Soldiers and Sailors Memorial Arch** is a Yankee arch of triumph (1898) that honors the Union victory in the Civil War. If you brave the heavy traffic, go up to the observation deck (below the four horse-drawn bronze chariot) for an aerial view; there may be an exhibition in the **Arch Gallery** (1-718-965-8999). Just outside the park, facing the Arch on Eastern Parkway, take a look at the sublime "Streamlined Beaux Arts" 1930s facade of Brooklyn Public Library.

Enter **Prospect Park at the Grand Army Plaza gate**; you will eventually make a large half-circle exiting at Prospect Park West into Park Slope at 9th St. Follow the path along the **Long Meadow**, where soccer and baseball games are usually in progress. Signs indicate the route to the **Music Pagoda** and the classical terrracotta Palladian style **Boathouse** which houses **the Audubon Visitor Center** (1-718-287-3400 for all activities; W-Th 1–5 F-Sun and holidays 10–5; free; maps and information; the café has a lovely view from the terrace). Here you may join a more extensive walking tour or rent a pedal boat ($10) for an hour. The electric launch **Independence** ($3) will take you for a 25 minute ride on the **Lake and Lullwater**. The latter has a sylvan beauty reminiscent of the Serpentine in London's Hyde Park. Just south is the weeping **Camperdown Elm**, called our "crowning curio" by beloved Brooklyn poet, Marianne Moore, who requested funds to save it rather than flowers at her funeral. Now, to complete the semi-circle that takes you to Prospect Park West, cross the Lullwater Bridge N of the Boathouse. Nearby, recently restored **Binnen Falls** is a popular picnic spot. As you meander NW towards the Lafayette Memorial/9th St. to exit into Park Slope, you'll pass within the park (to the right at 5th St.) the **Litchfield Villa.** Built for landed gentry in 1857, today it is an administrative center and home to the Prospect Park

Alliance (1-718-965-8951). **Montgomery Place** across the street has a concentration of very fine buildings.

Seasonal specials invite return trips. In winter, ski the perimeter, with beautiful brownstones in sight, or ice skate at Wollman Rink, overlooking the lake. On summer evenings, attend the **Celebrate Brooklyn Festival!**, a performance series offering a mix of music, dance, film and poetry in the **Bandshell**. Picnic under the stars at a performance of the New York Philharmonic Orchestra or the Metropolitan Opera; then watch fireworks (1-718-855-7882 for Brooklyn Information and Culture). Year round, weather permitting, join the happy circle in **Drummers Grove** (Ocean and Parkside; Sun afternoons) in singing, dancing, or playing an instrument. Cycle on designated paths.

For a return **children's day**, there is a convenient cluster of activities close to Flatbush Avenue. The brightly restored **Carousel** (S/Sun/holiday afternoons) contains antique pieces from early Coney Island carousels. Nearby is **Lefferts Homestead Children's Historic House Museum** (1-718-789-2822; weekends;12–4; cl. Aug; call for guided tour, F 10:30). **Prospect Park Wildlife Center** (450 Flatbush Ave.; 1-718-399-7339; www.wcs.org), where most bars have been removed, has interactive attractions like "**Animals in Art.**" **Imagination Playground** (Ocean Ave. and Lincoln Rd.) offers young children creative workshops and storytelling, Sat. afternoons.

Enter **Park Slope** at 9th St. on "**Prospect Park West,**" the "Gold Coast." Stroll by the parkside mansions; then thread the various beguiling side streets W towards **7th Ave.** 7th St. is a good block: Dutch gables give it a special warmth. Row houses throughout the area—individualized by cupolas, towers and turrets, stained glass and fanciful ornamentation—make for near perfect turn-of-the-century city blocks.

Hungry? Eating, shopping, and playing are not exclusive activities here. On **7th Ave.**, **Tea Lounge** (# 350) welcomes novice and grand master chess players with an enormous mahogany board inlaid into its own table and accompanied by oversized, elegantly carved chess pieces. Have a browse and a cappuccino at the **Community Book Store** (#143) where you can sit outside in the front garden near the fishpond. **The Clay Pot** (#162) has intriguing ceramics, and in **Leaf and Bean** (# 83), chocolate bars are at the standard one expects in "Chocolate City." **Cousin John's** (#70) is a tradition for breakfast, lunch, and gorgeous deserts. **Lemongrass Grill** (# 61A) is a favorite for Thai food. Across the street, **La Tacqueria's** (#72) burritos are really good. **Ozzie's Coffee** (# 57) has famous fresh lemonade; **2nd Street Café** (#189) offers a *prix fixe* dinner. A block west, on **6th Ave.**, **Rose Water** at Union St. is popular; come early for dinner. Further west, on 5th **Ave.**, among many newer cafes, bars, and restaurants, **Chip Shop** (#383) dishes up traditional Brit fish and chips; **Coco Roco** (#592; 1-718-965-3376) has Peruvian cuisine and dancing on some evenings. **Belleville** (5th and 5th; 1-718-832-9777) is new, French, and good.

Directions The #2/3 stop at Grand Army Plaza station in Brooklyn is close to Prospect Park and Park Slope. Cars are banned in Prospect Park on weekends and holidays and on weekdays, Apr-Nov, except between 5 and 7PM.

Want To Know More? Websites: info@prospectpark.org. See "The Complete Illustrated Guidebook to Prospect Park and the Brooklyn Botanic Garden," Berenson and deMause (2001). See the "AIA Guide to New York City" by White and Willensky (2000). The Hotline for general information including official trails is 1-718-965-8999

WALKING MAP

Queens Boulevard

①

Markwood Pl.

②

Metropolitan Ave.

Turnpike

East Main Drive

③

Myrtle Ave.

④

Wood Haven

South Park Lane

① Queens Blvd. Subway Exit

② Markwood Pl. entrance to Forest Hills Gardens

③ Forest Park's East Main Drive (no cars)

④ Woodhave Blvd. Crossing to Carousel

Green and Serene

Forest Hills Gardens and Forest Park

This delightful walk through **Forest Hills Gardens** and **Forest Park** is a lovely wooded escape from New York's skyscrapers any season of the year, but especially during Fall colors and Summer. Queens' most affluent section, Forest Hills Gardens boasts palatial brick, stone and stucco Tudor homes surrounded by mature trees and fronted by gardens in imitation of their English rural prototypes. After a stroll around the **Gardens' winding streets, Forest Park's woodland trails** and **traffic-free Forest Park Drive** take you to Master Carver Daniel Muller's 1903 **Carousel.** Carry a snack and then plan for a hearty meal at the end of the day in a Queens Boulevard **ethnic restaurant** or indulge in an old-fashioned hot fudge sundae in New York's most **charming ice cream parlor.**

The E/F train at the 75th St./Union Turnpike station (exit at 80th Rd./south side) is very close to **Forest Hills Gardens.** A few tranquil blocks off Queens Blvd. bring you to Park Lane, where a right turn takes you inside the Gardens' stone piers to Markwood Place. Amble around the winding, hilly streets; parking (BMWs and Mercedes only, please!) is by permit only, so the lanes are relatively car-free. Although the original 1909 plan envisioned the Gardens as a moderate income commuter community, the early residents "staged a coup" that revamped the project for exclusivity with single-family homes on large lots landscaped by Frederich Law Olmstead, Jr., the son of Central Park's architect. The ritzy West Side Tennis Club arrived here in

1913, but the US Open Tournaments moved to Flushing in 1977. Finish where you started at Markwood Place.

Forest Park's paved East/West Main Drive (approximately 3 miles rt.) begins just a few yards outside the Gardens' entrance piers. Maps are available at the Administrative Office on the hill, though you can hardly get lost without them. Yellow, red and blue loop trails (on signposts and tree blazes) lead off the East/West Drive into wooded areas where oak and tulip trees soar above you and bright red (male) cardinals streak through the branches. Diverging from the Yellow trail to the Red Trail, or staying on the Main Drive will take you to the Pine Grove, a delightfully odiferous "alley" with benches. As the **Main Drive** continues, it passes Victory Athletic Field (restrooms), and crosses Woodhaven Blvd. to the Visitor Center and beautifully carved **Carousel** (open approximately Apr-Oct). There is a small greenhouse behind the Carousel. The park-like environment soon ends and it's time to return to your starting point.

Hungry? Queens Boulevard, where you departed the subway, down to the next station, 71st and Continental now has a number of interesting ethnic restaurants reflecting the Russian, Balkan and Latin American population of the area. If you just feel like dessert, head for **Eddies Sweet Shop** (105–29 Metropolitan Ave; 1-718-520-8514) on the Q54 bus on Metropolitan Ave., which crosses Forest Park's East Drive near the beginning of the walk, in the direction towards Manhattan. Homemade ice cream treats in a kitschy 1940s setting (but not 40s prices) await you!

Directions E/F train to 75th St./Union Tpke Station; see walking directions to Forest Hills Gardens above. Return by the same subway lines on Queens Blvd. The return from Eddies Ice Cream Parlor requires a bus ride to Woodhaven Blvd. subway station.

Want To Know More? See Steve Reichstein's "Discovering Queens!" (2000); "If You're Thinking of Living In…" Times

Books (1999) and "A Modern Arcadia: Frederick Law Olmsted Jr. and the Plan for Forest Hills Gardens," Susan L. Klaus (2002).

WALKING MAP

❶ Entrance into
   Domestic Arts Building

❷ Souffle Cafe

❸ "The Nine Muses"

❹ Gazebo Cafe

❺ "If It Were Time" based
   on "Terrace at Saint Adresse"

Arcadia in Central New Jersey
The Grounds for Sculpture

The natural setting of **The Grounds for Sculpture**, a 22 acre botanical and sculpture garden in Hamilton, N.J. is so divine that it's well worth one and a half hour trip, by either car or train.

The Grounds for Sculpture is on the former New Jersey State Fair Grounds (18 Fairgrounds Road, open all year, T-Sat 10–9, 10–7 in Winter; $4, $10 Sun. Closed some holidays and for special events, call ahead 1-609-689-1089. The Museum and various exhibition buildings close at 4). Enter at the Art Deco Domestic Arts building (ca 1925), and pick up maps and checklists of the installations in the garden and on Sculptors' Way, the route leading to the Garden from the Hamilton train station, which is lined with 22 large scale creations including a modern, winged Don Quixote speeding full tilt towards a brilliant silver windmill.

The ambience of the Garden is so otherworldly, you may hear Pan playing pipes or glimpse handsome Narcissus yearning for the youth that is his own reflection in a dimpled pool, while the nymph, Echo, pines away out of unrequited love for him. Of course, we're speaking figuratively; many works in the garden are non-figurative and abstract. One of the day's joys is to find a meaning in a work, then check the title to see if your interpretation is "in synch" with the sculptor's thoughts.

Walking the garden is easy but extensive. The pathways, although intricate, have inviting rest areas. Children will love it but must be supervised, particularly in the water installations.

The rules are no food or drink from the outside; no music; no touching the sculptures or picking the flowers; no sports or pets; and **NO FEEDING THE PEACOCKS!**

In the garden you'll experience the seamless blending of antiquity and modernity. A striking abstract group, "The Nine Muses," evokes the classic marble statuary of Hadrian's Villa at Tivoli (ca 133 C.E.). The spirit of the muses is felt throughout the garden where the arts themselves—music, literature, poetry, painting, and dance—are sources of inspiration. Among the most enchanting sculptures are J. Seward Johnson, Jr.'s life-size figures adapted from familiar Impressionist paintings. These are placed in three-dimensional settings, some of which you can enter. Monet's "Terasse at Sainte Adresse," is created to life scale, but where the Monet "terasse" overlooks a turquoise blue English Channel, the terrace here opens onto a genuine New Jersey lake. Sound corny? it isn't; it's one more wonderful feature of this great escape.

Hungry? The Souffle Cafe (noon-3) offers good, inexpensive lunches. You may dine there in the interior air-conditioned space or alfresco, within view of the amorous couple from Renoir's "In the Garden: Under the Trees of Moulin de la Galatte." Light snacks are available at the **Gazebo Cafe**. Food can be taken to shaded picnic tables at the edge of a lovely pond. **Rats** (1-609-689-1089; reservations required) is also on the Grounds, open for dinner.

Directions By train: From Penn Station to Hamilton Station on the New Jersey Transit North East Corridor Line (1-973-762-5100; 1-973-378-6401; 1-800-772-2287 for schedule; round trip and senior fares, about $25; 75 minutes). The 5-minute taxi ride from Hamilton station, along Sculptor's Way is about $5. There is also an Amtrack train to Trenton (1-800-USA-RAIL).

By car: the Garden is off I-295, exit 63, 1 mile W on SR 33, .3 miles N on Ward Avenue Extension, 1 mile E. to 18 Fairgrounds Road (1½ hour).

Want To Know More? Meyer Schapiro, "Impressionism: Reflections and Perceptions" (1997); "Modern Art: 19th and 20th Centuries" (1978); "Sculpture of the Twentieth Century"; "Contemporary Outdoor Sculpture," Brooke Barrie (1999); and "Beyond the Frame: Impressionism Revisited," J. Seward Johnson, Jr.

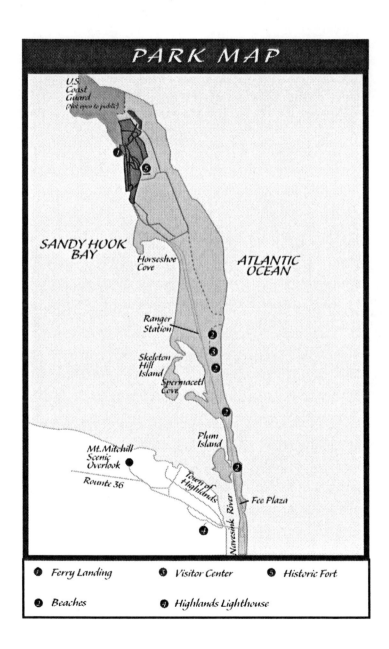

PARK MAP

U.S.
Coast
Guard
(Not open to public)

SANDY HOOK
BAY

ATLANTIC
OCEAN

Horseshoe
Cove

Ranger
Station

Skeleton
Hill
Island

Spermaceti
Cove

Plum
Island

Mt. Mitchill
Scenic
Overlook

Route 36

Town of
Highlands

Fee Plaza

Navesink River

❶	Ferry Landing	❸	Visitor Center	❺	Historic Fort
❷	Beaches	❹	Highlands Lighthouse		

A Beach with a View

The Ferry (or a drive) to Sandy Hook

When the first flat-bottomed canal boat, the Seneca Chief, arrived at New York's Battery on Nov. 4, 1825, its officials were asked, "Whence come you and where are you bound?" They answered, "From Lake Erie bound for Sandy Hook." The **Sandy Hook Unit** of Gateway National Recreation Area, which has had strategic importance in the defense of New York harbor since Colonial times, has, in addition to its many historical connections, **great swimming beaches** with a view of lower Manhattan. And getting there by **ferry** is more than half the fun! Sandy Hook is a refuge in the heart of the megalopolis of New York and New Jersey for many species of flora and fauna, including Homo Sapiens *au natural.* There is also a Visitor Center and **nature trails** which can be visited all year round, and a museum at Fort Hancock, where the ferry docks. A bike ride along the 6 mile stretch from one end of the Park to the other adds to the fun.

On Summer weekends, the **New York Waterway ferry** makes a 90 minute trip to Sandy Hook that offers spectacular views of lower Manhattan and passes under the Verrazano Bridge (1-800-533-3799; call for schedule. Reservations are a must; $25 rt. The ferry leaves twice a day from its 38th St. Dock on the Hudson River, around 9AM and 11AM and then picks up passengers at 9:30 and 11:30 at its Dock at the World Financial Center. Arrive at least 45 minutes ahead of schedule. Return trips are at 4:30PM and 6:00. Bikes are permitted for a small extra charge). A shuttle bus, free for ferry passengers, meets the ferry at the north end of Sandy Hook and makes stops at various beaches and visitor centers in the Park. At the north end, adjacent to the North Beach is a nude beach; a bikepath is being added. Further down the Hook, Beach Area E, is also is the site of the **Sandy Hook Visitor Center** (1-732 872-5970), with its interesting exhibits and maps for the nearby dune and beach walks. In addition to fast food beach concessions, there is also the **Seagulls Nest Restaurant**. The Recreation Area is open year round, dawn to dusk (beach parking fee $10.00 during Summer; otherwise parking is free).

At the very southern end of Sandy Hook is the town of Highlands, which has many seafood restaurants and the historic Sandy Hook lighthouse. Built high on a hill, in 1764, it is the oldest lighthouse in the United States. In Summer, the ferry also goes weekdays to Highlands, but keep in mind it's a long uphill walk to the lighthouse and a long hike to the Sandy Hook beaches and nature trails.

Directions By ferry (see above).

By car: Garden State Parkway to Exit 117, follow Route 36 East for 12 miles to the Park Entrance. Summer weekends get very crowded and the park closes when the parking lots are full. NJ Transit busses and trains (1-201-762-5100) go to Highlands, and there is also a bus to the Park Entrance. The Academy Busline goes from New York City to Highlands (1-212-564-8484).

Want To Know More? For more information on activities call 1-732-872-5970.

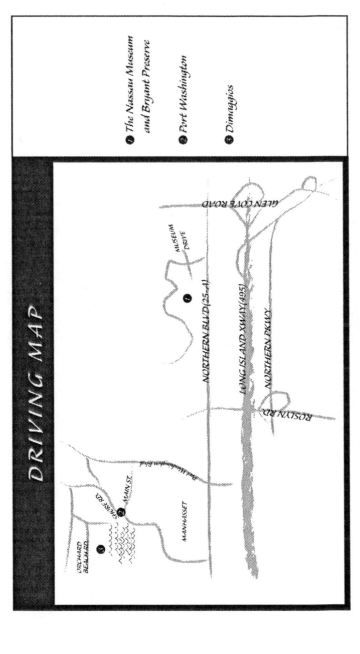

DRIVING MAP

1. The Nassau Museum and Bryant Preserve
2. Port Washington
3. Dimaggios

A Glorious Day of Art and Nature

The Nassau County Museum of Art

This day takes you to the very special **Nassau County Art Museum** for a glorious indoor and outdoor day of visual treats. In addition to their small permanent collection, the museum has excellent special exhibits, so you might want to **call ahead** for information. The Museum is set in the William Cullen Bryant Preserve, and contains an outdoor **Sculpture Garden**. Also on the grounds is the unique **Tee Ridder Museum of Miniatures.** The Museum has a small café for snacks, or you can bring your own lunch and eat in the garden. And whether you go by car (about 45 min. drive) or Long Island Railroad (about an hour), you have good options for a more substantial late lunch or an early dinner in nearby Long Island towns.

The main galleries of the **Nassau County Art Museum** (One Museum Drive, Roslyn Harbor, Long Island; 1-516-484-9338; T-Sun 11-5, Friday night 5–8; $4; free tours T-Sat.; a small café with simple meals; gift shop) are housed in a three story Georgian Mansion reflecting the Long Island Gold Coast architecture of the late 19th century. In Summer there is a free Sunday concert program at 3:30. Sign up at entry for reserved seating the day of the program and bring a blanket for lawn seating.

The museum is set within the **William Cullen Bryant Preserve** (9–5, no fee) a beautiful 145 acre sylvan treasure that contains **35 outdoor sculptures** sited to interact with the natural environment. The **Sculpture Garden** greets you first as you walk to the Museum. To make sure you see all the works, request a map at the museum entry desk. The sculptures are sited throughout the preserve, on the paved road leading from the parking lot to the museum and on the tree bordered meadows that surround the mansion. They are mostly massive abstracts of wood, steel, bronze and stone, but there are charming figurative pieces as well. One of our favorites is Jose Botero's ironic "Man on Horseback"; another is Chaim Gross's charming "The Hanneford Family Acrobats." Lunch in the shady glen behind the museum offers a view of the huge sculpture "Wooden Duck" reflected in the pond. A small **formal garden** on the grounds is restored to the original 1925 design commissioned by Frances Frick and designed by the well-known landscape architect, Marion Cruger Coffin.

The Tee Ridder Museum (free with Art Museum admission) is in a separate building beyond the Museum parking lot. Its enchanting exhibits of miniature rooms, created by Madelaine "Tee" Ridder, will delight adults and children alike. We were particularly enraptured by the Blue and White China room, and the African American miniature setting, evoking the setting of "Porgy and Bess".

Hungry? After your museum visit, there are some fine eating choices in the area. By car, the cute nearby town of Port Washington (see **Directions**) offers waterfront restaurants and cafes on Shore Road; locals especially like **Dimaggios** (Capri Marina & Yachting Center, Orchard Beach Blvd.; 1-516-944-5900). If you're returning by train, dinner at the **Chalet Restaurant and Bar,** two blocks from the railroad station on the left, is a good choice.

Directions By car: Long Island Expressway (the Northern State Parkway avoids the truck traffic) to exit 39 (Glencove Road), north to Rte. 25 A [Northern Blvd.], turn left; the museum/preserve is two lights down on the right (approx. 1 hour from midtown; free parking). To **Port Washington** from the museum, return to Northern Blvd., turn right on Pladome Rd, continue to Manorhaven Blvd., turn left to Orchard Beach Road, turn right into Orchard Beach Blvd. and the Yacht Center.

By LIRR (1-718-217-LIRR; call ahead for current schedule; the hourly trains take about 1 hour;, $10, cash only, at Penn Station. Pick up a schedule to select the time for your trip home. There may be a same-platform change at Jamaica. Exit at Roslyn Station where cabs are usually available [about $4 per person to the museum, including tip]; or call Deluxe Cabs [1-516-883-1900]). From the museum **call one half hour ahead for cab pickup back to the station.**

Want To Know More? "The Mansions of Long Island's Gold Coast," Monica Randall (1987). "The Gold Coast," Nelson DeMille (fiction, 1991).

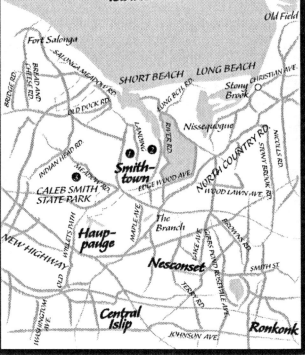

DRIVING MAP

LONG
ISLAND SOUND

Old Field

Fort Salonga

LONG ISLAND SOUND

SHORT BEACH   LONG BEACH

Stony
Brook   CHRISTIAN AVE.

Nissequogue

Smith-
town

Givens Park

The River

CALEB SMITH
STATE PARK

The
Branch

Haup-
pauge

Nesconset

Central
Islip

Ronkonk

JOHNSON AVE.

- **1** Givens Park
- **2** The River
- **3** Caleb Smith State Park

Paddle Your Own Canoe

Boating on the Nissequogue River

Active and outdoors, today's excursion is a **kayaking adventure** on the **Nissequogue River** and a nature walk in the nearby Caleb Smith State Park. You'll need a car for this all day trip, and bring your own lunch.

Even if you're a beginning kayaker, you won't be up the creek without a paddle on the scenic, placid Nissequogue River, now part of the new **Nissequogue River State Park**, in Smithtown, Long Island (open sunrise to sunset). As you glide along the 5.5 mile (one way) route to Long Island Sound, you'll pass a diverse riverine environment filled with herons, egrets, and migratory songbirds, as well as the endangered piping plover, who build their nests here. You'll sight many of these on the shore and in the large trees surrounding the river's inlets shoreline. Spring and Fall (from late August) are the bird migration seasons, which can be spectacular, and the Fall colors, in mid-late October, are stunning. A large sandbar on the route, or a picnic on Long Island Sound, are great lunch breaks on this easy paddling 2.5 hour round trip.

There are several kayak rental places for the Nissequogue. We've been very happy with Bob's (112 Whittier Drive, Kings Park; 1-631-269-9761, www.canoerentalslongisland.com; canoe rental $40, up to 3 people; single or double fiberglass kayaks are $40–50; life vests provided). Ask for the open kayaks with the back rest; wear shorts, a pair of shoes you won't mind getting wet, and bring a change of clothes. **Reservations are required, and**

you must call the night before to confirm the tides and times.
Weekdays, the one daily trip usually leaves between 10:30 and
11:00AM. **NO CREDIT CARDS:** cash or checks only. Bob's
also does moonlight trips and is open late Spring through Fall,
weather permitting. The Nissequogue River Canoe and Kayak
Club (1-631-979-8244) also does canoe and kayak trips similar
to Bob's. In the Summer you might want to start at Given Park
(see directions below) and head out to Long Island Sound, while
in the Fall, paddling up from King's Park gives the best views of
the Fall colors.

After the kayak trip, on the way back to the city, across from
Rte. 25 near Given Park, is the 543 acre **Caleb Smith State Park
Preserve** (1-631-265-1054; open all year 8AM to sunset), one
of the last undeveloped tracts of land on Long Island. The pretty
Fall colors (end Sept-early Oct), display the over 200 plant
species, including tulip trees, marsh marigold and skunk cab-
bage. There are two short, easy, self-guiding nature trails (1 mile
or 2½ mile options) from the Jericho Turnpike (Rte 25)
entrance. Just down the road is a Friendlys where you can snack
up before heading back to the city.

Directions LIE to exit 53 N (Sunken Meadow Parkway
North) (or LIE to the Grand Central which becomes the
Northern State, no trucks) to exit 3 E on the Sunken Meadow
Parkway, which puts you on Rte 25, the Jericho Turnpike. Keep
going about 4 miles on Jericho Turnpike to the sign that says
"Welcome to Smithtown." Behind this sign is a small sign that
says "Paul Given Park." Turn in to the dirt driveway and you'll
see the vans with the kayaks getting ready for the trip to King's
Park (about 1½ hours from lower Manhattan). For King's Park,
take Exit 4E (Pulaski Road Eastbound) on the Sunken Meadow
Parkway, continue 3 miles to where it ends at the foot of Old
Dock Road at the water's edge.

Want To Know More? "Wetlands," William Niering,
Audubon Society Nature Guides (1985); Nissequogue River
State Park, Kings Park, L.I. 1-631-269-4927.

DRIVING MAP

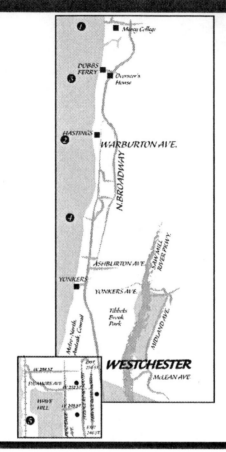

- ❶ VE Macy Park
- ❷ Harvest on Hudson
- ❸ Chart House
- ❹ Hudson River Museum
- ❺ Wavehill

An Eyeful of Beauty

Pond Walk, Hudson Views and the Hudson River Museum

This day includes a lovely lakeside walk at **V.E. Macy Park**, **lunch with dramatic Hudson River views**, a visit to the **Hudson River Museum of Westchester,** featuring the work of whimsical artist Red Grooms, and a stop at the unique **Wave Hill** garden for more Hudson River vistas. Beautiful any time of year, the Fall colors make these sites a special seasonal treat. The whole day can only be done by car, but some segments are also accessible by public transportation.

The day begins with a walk along the **Woodlands Lake** at V.E. Macy Park (free parking), an area that was part of the Philipsburg Manor (now an historic site in Tarrytown) in the 17th and 18th centuries. From 1888 to 1958, the Putnam Division of the New York Central Railroad (called "Old Put") ran north between the Bronx and Brewster to towns in Westchester County. In the late 19th century the Woodlands Lake Station served the Woodlands Lake Hotel, a resort for New York City's elite, who swam and rowed on the lake in Summer and skated on it through the Winter. Later, the area was a dairy farm owned by J.P. Morgan and the abandoned hotel building was used for ice and sawdust storage. Ultimately, the resort lawns became a public park. With the demise of the railroad, the line was converted into a "rails to trails" bicycle and pedestrian path for several miles in both directions from Macy Park. The trail is marked by informative signposts describing some of the stations.

Hungry? After your walk, you can enjoy a lovely lunch or brunch in one of the many towns along the Hudson River. A short drive south brings you to **Harvest on Hudson** (1 River St., Hastings; 1-914 478-2800, M-F 11:30–3), a transformed beer factory with indoor and outdoor dining, great views and delicious food (and an adjacent children's playground). On Sundays only, brunch is available at the **Chart House** restaurant (foot of High Street on the water in Dobbs Ferry, adjacent to the Dobbs Ferry Metro North train station; 1-914-693-4130; noon–3).

After lunch, treat yourself to the small **Hudson River Museum of Westchester** (511 Warburton Ave; 1-914 963-4550; W-Sun noon–5; F eve free, cl. major holidays; $3-5). Overlooking the Hudson, the Museum houses a small Americana collection, but its highlight is the "bookstore and gift shop" by Red Grooms, America's "antic architect" known for his whimsical life-sized human figures and sculptured environments. Here you can "browse," with other life-sized, stuffed vinyl "customers" in a "bookstore" that combines the elegance of the Morgan Library with the funkiness of the (now closed) old booklover's mecca, the Isaac Mendoza bookstore in lower Manhattan. Adjacent to the Museum is the John Bond Trevor Glenview Mansion, a meticulously preserved late 19th century chateau,

Wave Hill (W. 249th St. and Independence Ave, Riverdale section of the Bronx; 1-718-549-3200, www.wavehill.org, T-Sun 10–4:30; $2–4; free T and from Nov 15-Mar 15; free parking) is a public garden and cultural institution dedicated to making "connections between people and nature." Its divine grounds, with dramatic views of the Palisades across the Hudson River, contain a greenhouse, art gallery, shop, and café. The site hosts many cultural events during fine weather. As you drive in, on your left, notice the Telshe Yeshiva, a small branch of a famous Chicago Yeshiva, named for the Lithuanian town where it originated.

Directions By car: For Macy Park, take the FDR to the Major Deegan, to Sawmill River Parkway north, Exit 19; about

45 min. from lower Manhattan. For Harvest on Hudson, return south on the Sawmill, take Exit 12, Farragut Parkway, 1 mile to the 5-way intersection, turn left down the hill on Main St., continue ¼ mile to the light, turn right on Warburton Ave., go 100 yards, turn left on Southside Ave (also called Maple St.) and go 100 yards to the Hastings Train Station. Turn right over the bridge adjacent to the train station and turn right again on the other side of the bridge on River St. The restaurant is 300 yards ahead. For the Chart House from Macy Park, also return to the Sawmill Parkway south, follow signs to the Dobbs Ferry Train Station, go left, down to the water. For the Hudson River Museum from Hastings, go back to Warburton Avenue and continue south to the Museum. To reach Wave Hill, take the Sawmill Parkway to the Henry Hudson Parkway south, exit at 254th St. (signs for Wave Hill). Turn left at the stop sign, then left at the light. Make a right at 249th St. to the Wave Hill gate.

By public transportation: to the Harvest on Hudson or Chart House restaurants, take Metro North (1-212-532-4900 for schedules to both Hastings and Dobbs Ferry) and walk or taxi down to the waterfront. To Wave Hill, take Metro North to Riverdale Station, and walk uphill to the entrance. Also, Liberty Lines Express Bus (1-718-652-8400) from Manhattan (short uphill walk to gate); A train to 207th St. stop/connecting Bx7 bus (walk to gate).

Want To Know More? "Knights of the Brush: the Hudson River School and the Moral Landscape," James F. Cooper (1999); "The Hudson River and its Painters," John K. Howat (1978); "The Art of Thomas Cole: Ambition and Imagination," Ellwood Parry III (1988); "Red Grooms: the Graphic Work," Walter Knestrick (2001).

DRIVING MAP

SCARBOROUGH

SCARBORO RD.

SLEEPY HOLLOW RD.

❶ Rockefeller State Park Preserve

N. BROADWAY

Sleepy Hollow Cemetery

❺

Philipsburg manor

❷ BEDFORD RD.

TARRYTOWN
❻

TAPPAN ZEE BRIDGE

❸

❹

---

❶ Rockefeller Preserve   ❹ Sunnyside

❷ Union Church   ❺ Old Dutch Church

❸ Lyndhurst   ❻ Restaurants

Tarrying in Tarrytown

The Rockefeller Preserve, Historic Tarrytown and Sleepy Hollow Country

You'll want to tarry at each stop on this perfect day just north of New York City. A lovely drive takes you to an easy lakeside hike in the **Rockefeller Preserve, lunch in historic Tarrytown** on the Hudson, the art-filled **Union Church** in Pocantico Hills, and a choice of visits to several **historic houses**. The whole day is conveniently accessible only by car but with some walking, the Tarrytown restaurants and historic houses can be accessed by Metro North (see Directions).

The day begins at the serene, unspoiled 750 acre **Rockefeller State Park Preserve** (1-914-631-0338; daily year round; $5 vehicle fee weekends/summer; waived weekdays for over 62). The preserve, designed for quiet walking, seems so secluded it's hard to believe towns and highways are just around the corner. There are many walks in diverse environments—woods, wetlands, and riverside lanes—in this Hudson valley landscape, so you can choose the one (or more) that suits your mood. To start out, obtain the map provided at the Visitor Center. There are only a few picnic tables at the preserve entrance and picnicking is not permitted within the preserve itself, so save lunch for Tarrytown.

With lots to do later, the 1.5 mile walk around the Preserve's **Swan Lake** is a perfect way to start the day. Ducks and turtles abound in the lake and birds in the trees; you may even see one of the giant tortoises mosey up the path. The easy trails (there is one uphill for Hudson views) criss-cross each other, leaving many choices for return trips. This is a park for all seasons and especially nice for Winter walks. Weekdays you're likely to have the place to yourself, and even on weekends it's mostly local residents walking the (leashed) dogs or gathering in the lower parking lot to wash their horses.

Hungry? Many Tarrytown restaurants and the snack places lining Broadway, the main street (Rte 9) offer tasty food (metered parking). **Horsefeathers** (94 N. Broadway; 1-914-631-6606; M-Sat all day, Sun 5–9) has good, reasonable, homestyle food in a cozy atmosphere. Main St., west of Broadway at the south end of town, also has many restaurants, such as **Isabel's Café** (61 Main St., open daily, lunch specials); or the **Main Street Café** (24 Main St.; closed Mon., lunch 12–3). Or you may like to head west to the Hudson for waterside dining at **The Striped Bass** (behind Tarrytown RR station; 1-914-366-4455, open daily, free parking) is often crowded at lunchtime, so try the fine **Sunset Cove** Restaurant just beyond it, also on the water.

After lunch, turn north again on Rte 9 just north of Tarrytown (turnoff at Rte 448, Bedford Road), take a right and follow the signs for your visit to the **Union church at Pocantico** (1-914-631-8200; W/Th/F 11-5; Sun, Apr–Dec 2-4; $4). Nestled in a pretty village, this lovely ivy-covered church is adorned with several pieces of art commissioned by the Rockefellers, including stained glass windows by Marc Chagall and a window by Henri Matisse.

After visiting this 19th century church, you can explore other aspects of Tarrytown's past by visiting one of its **historic buildings**. The Tarrytown region was first inhabited by the Weckquasgeek Indians. In 1609 Henrick Hudson claimed it for the Dutch, who settled there and remained even after the English took over in 1664. The Dutch influence can still be seen in the 17th century **Old Dutch Church** (north of Tarrytown on the right, Rte 9), maintained by the same Dutch reform congregation which settled there in 1697. Its surrounding burial ground includes gravestones of early Dutch settlers and many of the characters found in Washington Irving's "The Legend of Sleepy Hollow." Following the American Revolution, the Tarrytowns flourished as a center of business and industry and before long wealthy industrialists from New York City established palatial estates along the Hudson. One of these, just north of Tarrytown, is **Philipsburg Manor** (Upper Mills, N. Tarrytown; 1-914-631-3992, closed T; entrance fees vary), a restored (some say over-restored) 18th century farm and trading center, with live animals, a gift shop and café.

If you continue south of Tarrytown on Rte 9, there are two historic homes with special appeal. **Sunnyside** (West Sunnyside Lane, Tarrytown, near the Hudson; 1-914-591-8763; Open Mar-Dec 10-5, closed T and major holidays in Winter; Tours $9), is the picturesque restored home of Washington Irving. It remains much as it appeared in the last years of his life, including the original furnishings and personal possessions and you can see the views of Tappen Zee that he loved so much. Nearby is the majestic **Lyndhurst** (635 Broadway, Tarrytown, 1-914-631-4481; open May-Oct, and Dec, daily except Mon. and major holidays 10-5. Call for hours at other seasons; Guided tours $7; Carriage House Café offers lunch in summer), a masterpiece of 19th century Gothic Revival architecture, was owned by railroad speculator Jay Gould and is chock full of treasures: furniture, Tiffany glass, silver, rugs, fine paintings and trompe l'oeil designs. The Rockefeller's estate, Kykiut, is also nearby but we'll leave that for another perfect day.

Directions By car: FDR to Major Deegan north (it becomes the New York State Thruway, to Exit 9, to Rte. 9 North, through Tarrytown and North Tarrytown. Turn right on Rte 117 and follow signs to Rockefeller Preserve [under one hour]). To return to Tarrytown, go back the way you came; driving south on Rte 9 you pass Philipsburg Manor; nearby on the left, is the turnoff for the Union Church (Rte 448, Bedford Road; you'll see signs for the Church). Rte. 9, where the restaurants are located, becomes N. Broadway in Tarrytown; the Main Street and waterside restaurants require a right turn on Main St. To visit Sunnyside or Lyndhurst, continue south on Rte 9 about ½ mile past the Thruway (Rte 287) at the Tappan Zee Bridge.

By train: In season, Metro-North (1-800-638-7646 for schedules) offers rail/van excursions to the sites on weekends. Otherwise you'll have a couple of miles walk from the Tarrytown train station, or you can take a taxi (1-914-631-TAXI, approx. $3 per person).

Want To Know More? Washington Irving, "The Legend of Sleepy Hollow"; Maury Klein, "The Life and Legend of Jay Gould" (1986); Alexis Gregory, "Families of Fortune: Life in the Gilded Age" (1993); Joy Hakim, "An Age of Extremes" (1994); Ron Chernow, "Rockefeller" (2000). Also, Historic Hudson Valley 1-914-631-8200; www. hudsonvalley.org

Appendix A

One Perfect Day

Only one day in the city? You can't see everything, but this one perfect day helps you make the most of your time. Choose either our West Side or East Side route, and you'll be seeing New York—its places and people—on your own, in an efficient, organized way at your own pace. To begin the day, choose the upper West Side or upper East Side option, both of which introduce you to New York's fabulous museums and allow a stroll through our divine Central Park. If you're most inclined to science, anthropology or cultural history, and especially if you have children with you, take the West Side option, and begin at the fantastic **American Museum of Natural History** (79th St. and Central Park West; 1-212-769-5100; open daily 10–5:30; sugg. Adm.; excellent cafeteria and gift shops). Enjoy its fabulous dinosaurs, new Milstein Family **Hall of Ocean Life**, children's Discovery Room, Halls of Asian, African, South American and Native American peoples or a visit to the stars at the Rose Planetarium. Adjacent is the **New York Historical Society** (2 W. 77th/CPW; 1-212-873-3400; T-Sun 10-6, M; $6), with a permanent Americana collection and marvelous display of Tiffany lamps, as well as its magnificent exhibition of 9/11 memorabilia, films and photographs.

If your interests run to fine art, take the East Side option and head for **Museum Mile** on upper Fifth Avenue, where there are many outstanding collections. At 92nd and Fifth is the **The Jewish Museum** (1109 5th Ave./92 nd St.; 1-212-423-3200; $7.50-10; Sun-W 11-5; F 11-3; Th eve til 8; donation). At 1071

5th Ave./89th is the ultra-modern **Guggenheim** (1-212-423-
3500; 9:00–6, Sat-W 10-5; F til 8; $10-15). A few blocks down,
at 1048 5th Ave./86th is the newest addition to our arts scene,
the **Neue Galerie New York** (1-212-628-6200; Fri 11-9; Sat-M
11–6; $10), with German and Austrian art and a re-creation of
a European Café. The incomparable **Metropolitan Museum of
Art** (Fifth at 82nd; 1-212-535-7710; T-Th/Sun 9:30-5:30; F-
Sat 9:30-9PM; suggested adm.), is the home to paintings and
sculpture that traverse the centuries and the globe, as well as the
Michael Rockefeller Room of tribal art, a fantastic Egyptian
Collection, a new Greek corridor, and even an outdoor roof
sculpture garden open seasonally (cafeteria and restaurant). For
an intimate experience of fine art in a lovely house museum,
visit **The Frick Collection** (1 E.70th St.; 1-212-288-0700;
$5–12; no children under 10; 10–6, cl. Sun. mornings and M).

After a morning at the Museums, whether you've chosen the
East Side or the West Side alternative, amble through **Central
Park** down to 59th St., to the Park Plaza Hotel, with its grand
fountain and horses and carriages parked alongside. Stroll and
window shop down Fifth Avenue, with its elegant shops, to
48th St. for a view of **Rockefeller Center** (in winter its delightful skating rink may even tempt you to try your skills on the
ice). **Hungry?** There are lots of informal eating places in the subway level of Rockefeller Arcade or even in its own elegant (and
not too too expensive) restaurant. Continue walking down Fifth
Avenue (or take the bus) to 34th St. for your trip to the top of
the **Empire State Building** and its observation tower for spectacular city views. If you can hold out for **lunch**, there are good,
inexpensive places at your next stop, Greenwich Village.

From just in front of the Empire State Building, continue on
the Fifth Avenue Bus downtown to **Washington Square Park**,
where you'll see one of the funkier gathering places of
Greenwich Village. Walk south through the park and you'll be
heading right into **SOHO**, with its art galleries and ultra-trendy
boutiques (you'll be on West Broadway here). **Hungry?** West

Broadway between the Park and Soho offers plenty of small, good restaurants. After strolling through Soho, anytime your feet give out, turn left for three short blocks and take the Broadway bus down to **Ground Zero.** Exit the bus at Fulton St., and turn right to view the site, which is in the process of reconstruction. From there you can continue west to the **Hudson River Pedestrian Path** (if you're running out of time, return to Broadway and take the bus) to **Battery Park** with its many memorials and adjacent **Staten Island Ferry** for one of the greatest free rides you'll ever have. On the ½ hour trip over and back you'll see the **Statue of Liberty** and **Ellis Island** in the distance, as well as the exhilarating views of the downtown New York skyline and harbor.

Back at Battery Park, walk to the #6 subway at Bowling Green and ride uptown to the Canal Street stop. This will give you the option of shopping and eating in **Chinatown** (to the south) or **Little Italy** (to the north; for restaurant suggestions, see Strangers to our Shores Day). From either Chinatown or Little Italy you can hop on the BMT subway train uptown to **Times Square**, where you'll get the electric night view of the kinetic signs and sights that make this the most dynamic entertainment center in the world. And, if you can still keep your eyes open, try the **TKS Booth** at Broadway and 46th St. for half-price, last minute tickets to a **Broadway show!**

Appendix B

New York City Special Events

JANUARY

January 1: St. Mark's in the Bowery Church Marathon Poetry Reading: 2nd Ave./10th St.; 2PM-Midnight; 1-212-674-0910/6377; #6 train to Astor Place

January 1: Coney Island Polar Bear Club New Years Swim: Coney Island Beach; 1PM; 1-718-372-5159 (Coney Island USA) for details; Q train to Brighton Beach or F to W. 8th St.

January 6: Three Kings Day Parade: 3rd Ave. from 106th-116th Sts.; starts at 106th St./5th Ave.; 1-212-831-7272 (Museum of the Barrio); #6 train to 103rd St.

Mid-January: Outsider Art Fair at the Puck Building: 295 Lafayette/Jersey Sts.; 1-212-274-8900/777-5218 for exact date; #6 train to Spring St., N/R to Prince St. or F to Bway-Lafayette St.

Late January: Winter Antiques Show at the Seventh Regiment Armory: Park Ave./67th St.; 1-718-665-5250; www.winterantiquesshow.com (for exact date, fees); #6 train to 68th St.

FEBRUARY

Late January/Early February: Chinese New Years Parade: Chinatown 3rd Ave./Mott/Mulberry Sts.; 1-212-566-1377 (Wan Chi Ming Institute) or 1-212-233-2154 (Asian American Arts Center) for exact date and time; #6 or N/R train to Canal St.

MARCH

March to May: Texuba Kimono Show: (moveable date/place); 1-310-827-8535; www texuba.com.

March 17: St. Patrick Day's: Try an alternate LGBT Parade: check Gay City News or website: www.GayCityNews.com.

Easter Sunday (March/April): Easter Parade: 5th Ave./Rockefeller Center-47th St. to Central Park; F or Q train to Rockefeller Center/47th St.

APRIL

Mid-April Weekend: Brooklyn Botanic Gardens Sakura Matsuri/Cherry Blossom Festival 900 Washington Ave.; 1-718-622-7200 for date; #2/3 train to Eastern Pkwy

Mid-April: Branch Brook Park Cherry Blossom Festival, Newark: 1-973-643-1611x139; www.branchbrookpark.org for date/events/directions; PATH train to Penn Station, Newark; transfer to Newark City Subway, direction Franklin; exit Branch Brook Park station: cross tracks and uphill to Grafton Ave., turn left and continue to Visitor Center Bldg.(on right). Follow path behind Center about ½ mile, cross road and walk along stream for the Cherry trees. Stroll about ¼ mile, cross the bridge, return the same way at the first major intersection, Mt. Prospect Ave.
By car: Rte#280 W; from Newark Exit 13, go West on Central Ave. (towards Cathedral); turn into Park; take Park road about 2 miles north to sign "Cherry Blossom Rte.;" free parking in Visitor Center lot.

Mid-April: Prospect Heights Historic District House Tour: 1-718-859-3800 (Flatbush Development Corporation for date, fees;) Q train to Church Ave.

April 30: George Washington Inaugural Reenactment: Federal Hall 25 Wall St./corner Broad; 11:30AM; 1-212-825-6888; #2/3 train to Wall St., N/R to City Hall or #4/5 to Bway-Nassau/Fulton St. station

MAY

1st Sunday: Cuban Day Parade: 6th Ave./44th St.-Central Park; 1-212-348-2100 (Nick Lugo Travel); F train to Rockefeller Center-47th St.

Moveable Mid-May to Mid-June weekends: Red Hook Waterfront Arts Festival of the Brooklyn Working Artists Coalition (BWAC): Pier Show at 499 Van Brunt St. (a Civil War warehouse on the water); 1-718-596-2507; www.bwac.org; F or G train to Smith-9th Sts. and transfer to B77 bus to Van Dyke/Van Brunt Sts. or A/C/F trains to Jay St.-Borough Hall and transfer to B61 bus to Van Dyke/Van Brunt Sts.

May 14: Salute to Israel Parade: 5th Ave./57th-59th Sts.; noon; 1-212-644-2663; B train to 57th St, #4/5 to 59th St. or N to 60th St.

Weekend after Mother's Day: 9th Avenue International Food Festival: 9th Ave./37th-57th Sts.; 11-7; 1-212-581-7217 (Ninth Avenue Association); A/C train to 34th or 59th Sts.

3rd Sunday: Sheepshead Bay Blessing of the Fleet: Emmons Ave./E. 26th St.; 2-5PM; 1-718-646-9206 (a Bay improvement group); Q train to Sheepshead Bay stop

JUNE

Sunday Near June 14: Puerto Rican Day Parade: 5th Ave./44th-86th Sts.; noon; 1-212-348-2100 (Nick LugoTravel); F train to Rockefeller Center/47th St.

Saturday Nearest June 21: Mermaid Parade: Coney Island, Surf Ave.; 2PM; 1-718-372-5159 (Coney Island USA); N train to Stillwell Ave. (last stop)

Sunday Late-June: Lesbian and Gay Pride Parade: 5th Ave./midtown south to Greenwich Village; noon; 1-212-807-7433 (Heritage Pride Inc.)

JULY

1st & 2nd Sunday: Feast of the Giglio: North 8th/Havermeyer Sts., Williamsburg; 1st Sun; 1PM/2nd Sun:2PM; 1-718-384-0223 (Our Lady of Mt. Carmel); A/C train to 14th St.; transfer to L train to Lorimer St.; walk 3 blocks

July 4th: Fireworks: East River (check local papers)

Sunday Mid-July: Japanese O Bon Festival: Bryant Park; 1–4PM; 1-212-678-0305/9213 (New York Buddhist Church of Riverside Drive); F train to 42nd St.

AUGUST

Sunday Mid-August: Arthur Avenue Ferragosto: Arthur Ave, Bronx; 1-718-881-8900 (Bronx Historical Society) or 1-718-590-3500 (Bronx Borough President's Office); B/D/#4 train to Fordham Rd. and transfer to Bx12 bus.

Moveable: Macy's Tap-0-Mania: Macy's Herald Square; noon (registration to tap 8–10:30AM; 1-212-494-4400/4495); all west side trains to 34th St.

Weekend Mid-August: Hong Kong Dragon Boat Races: Flushing Meadows-Corona Park 1-718-760-6565 or 1-212-751-4659 (Hong Kong Economic Trade Office); #7 train to Shea Stadium

3 Weeks In August: Harlem Week: various sites and events including Rucker Playground "Entertainers League" basketball tournament 1-212-427-7200 (Greater Harlem Chamber of Commerce). transportation will vary

SEPTEMBER

Labor Day: Labor Day Parade: no longer an annual NYC event, check newspapers for details **Labor Day to 1st Weekend: West Indian Day Carnival:** Eastern Parkway/Grand Army Plaza to Utica Ave., Brooklyn; 1-718-625-1515 or 1-718-638-5000 (Brooklyn Museum); #3/4 train to Utica Ave.

1st Weekend: Richmond Historic Town Restauration County Fair: St. Patrick's Place; 11–7; $3–6 fee; 1-718-351-1611/1617; Staten Island Ferry and transfer to S54 or S74 bus

Labor Day Weekend: Wigstock: Pier 54 on West St. between 12th-13th Sts.; 2–10PM; fee, but standing at the entrance to see the fabulously costumed folks is free; see Village Voice newspaper for details;A/C/E/L trains to 14th St./8th Ave.

Labor Day Weekend: La Bombazo Afro-Puerto Rican Festival: Brook Ave./158th St., Bronx; 1-212-788-8065 (Green Thumb); #2/5 train to Jackson Ave.

1st Sunday: Brazilian Street Festival: "Little Brazil" W. 46th St. Madison Ave.-Bway; 9–6; 1-212-751-4691 (Brazilian American Chamber of Commerce); all trains to 42nd St.

11 Days in Mid-September: Feast of San Gennaro: Mulberry St. From Canal-Houston Sts.; 11:30AM-11:30PM; 1-212-768-9320 (Figli Di San Gennaro, Inc.) or 1-212-226-6427 (Church of the Most Precious Blood); #6 or N/R train to Canal St.

September 30: Atlantic Antic: Atlantic Ave. between Hicks St.-4th Ave., Brooklyn; 10–6; 1-718-875-8993; N/R, #2/3/4 trains to Borough Hall

OCTOBER

1st Sunday in October: Feast of St. Francis "Blessing of the Animals": Cathedral of St. John the Divine;1047Amsterdam Ave./ 112th St.;1-212-316-7540; #1/9 train to Cathedral Pkwy-110th

A Sunday in October, Moveable: Uptown Treasures: A Day of Art, Music and History: various sites in Inwood and Washington Heights; 1-212-696-7995 (Uptown Treasures); www.uptowntreasures.org; #2/3/1/9 and A trains (will vary by site)

Monday Close to October 11: Columbus Day Parade: 5th Ave./44th St. to 79th St.; noon; N/R/#4/5/6 trains to 42nd St. or 59th St.; #6 to 77th St.–walk to Fifth

Early October: Tibetan Festival: Tibetan Museum; 338 Lighthouse Ave., Staten Island; noon-5; 1-718-987-3500; Staten Island Ferry and transfer to S74 bus

October 31: New York's Greenwich Village Halloween Parade: Houston St.-14th St.; 7PM; (see Village Voice newspaper for details); F train to Bway-Lafayette or N/R to Prince St.

NOVEMBER

Early November: New York City Marathon: from the Staten Island side of the Verrazano Bridge through all 5 boroughs finishing at Central Park and W. 67th St. (Tavern on the Green); 1-212-860-46577/4476 (Road Runners Club)

Thanksgiving: Macy's Thanksgiving Day Parade: Central Park West from 77th St.-59th on CPW/then to 34th on Bway; the evening before, the giant balloons are blown up on the streets near the Museum of Natural History (81st/CPW)

DECEMBER

All Month: Bronx Zoo Illumination of the Animals on Tree of Life: Zoo's Fountain Circle Main Gate at junction of Fordham Rd. and Pelham Pkwy; 1-718-220-5100 (call for hours, fees); closest train to Main Gate is #2 to Pelham Park-White Plains Rd.

Around Christmas: Holiday Decorations on Dyker Heights Homes: Dyker Heights, Brooklyn; R train to 86th St.

Sunday near Christmas: Blessing of the Animals and their Families: Park Ave. United Methodist Church; 106 E. 86th St. between Park-Lexington Aves.; 1-212-427-5421 for details; #4/5/6 trains to 86th St.

December 31: Central Park Fireworks: best views are Central Park/72nd St., Central Park West/67th St., and 5th Ave./90th St.

December 31: New Year's Eve Midnight Run: starts at Tavern on the Green at Central Park West/67th St.; 1-212-860-6577/4476 (Road Runners Club); B/C trains to 72nd St. or #1/9 to 66th St.-Lincoln Center

December 31: New Year's Eve Lowering of the Glittering Sphere in Times Square: 42nd/Bway; crowds gather early; sphere drops at Midnight; #1/9/2/3/A/C trains to Times Square

Appendix C

Want to Know More?

NEW YORK CITY BOOKS, WALKING TOURS AND WEBSITES

BOOKS

"AAA Guide to New York City," Norval White and Elliot Willensky (2002)

"Art and the Empire City: New York, 1825–1861," Catherine Hoover Vorsanger and John K. Howat, eds. (2002)

"At Sea in the City: New York from the Water's Edge," William Kornblum (2002)

"Brooklyn: A State of Mind: 125 Original Stories from America's Most Colorful City," Michael Robbins (2001)

"Empire City: New York Through the Centuries," Kenneth T. Jackson and David S. Dunbar, eds. (2002)

"The Encyclopedia of New York City," Kenneth T. Jackson (1995)

"Gotham: A History of New York City to 1898," Edwin G. Burrows and Mike Wallace (1999)

"Harlem Lost and Found: An Architectural and Social History" Micheal Adams (2003)

"A Hazard of New Fortunes," William Dean Howells (1890; reprinted 2002)

"Harpo Speaks…about New York," Harpo Marx (2001)

"Here is New York," E.B. White (1949; reprinted 1999)

"The Historic Shops & Restaurants of New York," Ellen Williams & Steve Radlauer (2002)

"Joseph Cornell: Master of Dreams," Diane Waldman (2002)

"Julius Knipl, Real Estate Photographer," Ben Katchor (1996)

"Knickerbocker's History of New York," Washington Irving (1809)

"Low Life: Lures and Snares of Old New York," Luc Sante (1991)

"Manhattan Block by Block: A Street Atlas," John Tauranac (2000)

"The Monied Metropolis: New York City and the Consolidation of the American Bourgeoisie, 1850–1900," Sven Beckert (2001)

MUSEUMS NEW YORK (quarterly handbook available free at many museums)

"A New Deal for New York," Mike Wallace (2002)

"New Immigrants in New York," Nancy Foner, ed. (1987)

"New York: Capital of Photography" Max Kozloff (2002)

"New York City Trees: A Field Guide for the Metropolitan Area," Edward Barnard (2002)

"New York Living Rooms," Dominique Nabokov (1998)

"NEW YORK: Songs of the City," Nancy Groce (1999)

"New York's 50 Best Art in Public Places," David Masello (1999)

"The Novel of New York" (5 historical novels), Bruce Nicolaysen (1980s)

"One Thousand New York Buildings," Bill Harris (2000)

"On Night's Shore," Randall Silvis (2001)

"Picturing New York: The City from its Beginnings to the Present," Gloria Deak (2000)

"This Place on Third Avenue: The New York Stories of John McNulty," John McNulty (2001)

"The Power Broker: Robert Moses," Robert Caro (1974)

"Privately Owned Public Space: The New York City Experience," Jerold Kayden (2000)

"A Short Remarkable History of New York City," Jane Mushabac and Angela Wigan (1999)

"Style and Grace: African Americans in Harlem,: Micheal Adams (2003)

"Time and Again," Jack Finney (1970)

"Unearthing Gotham," Anne-Marie Cantwell and Diana diZerega Wall (2001)

"The Ungovernable City: John Lindsay and His Struggle to Save New York," Vincent J. Cannato (2001)

"Walking the Hudson: Batt to Bear: From the Battery to Bear Mountain," Cy Adler (1997)

"Walking Manhattan's Rim: The Great Saunter," Cy Adler (2003)

"Writing New York," Phillip Lopate (1998)

NYC WALKING TOURS

Audio CD Walking Tours in Manhattan and the Bronx www. SoundWalk.com

Micheal Henry Adams (art and architecture/Harlem) 1-212-426-5757

Big Onion Walking Tours 1-212-439-1090; www.bigonion.com

Bronx Historical Society 1-718-881-8900
www.bronxhistoricalsociety.org

Harlem Spirituals, Inc. 1-212-390-0900

Harlem Your Way Tours Unlimited 129 W. 130th St. 1-212-690-1687

Municipal Art Society of New York 457 Madison Ave. NYC 10022 1-212-935-3960 www.mas.org 92nd St. YMCA 1-212-996-1100

Shorewalkers (city walks/nearby hikes) 1-212-330-7686; Shorewalkers.org

NYC TOURIST INFORMATION/WEBSITES

Brooklyn Information and Culture, Inc. 1-718-855-7882
www.brooklynx.org

Brooklyn Arts Council 1-718-625-0080

City Lore www.citylore.org (cultural/ethnic events)

Manhattan Chamber of Commerce 1-212-479-7772

Mayor's Website for neighborhood residents' information
www.nyc.gov/mmr

Manhattan Getaways Metro-North 1-212-532-4900
www.mta.nyc.ny.us

MTA Travel Information Center 1-718-330-1234 (reliable transit
information/specific routes)

New York City Convention and Visitors Bureau 1-212-484-1222
www.nycvisit.com

NYC Visitor Information Center 810 7th Ave./53rd St. 1-800-
NYC-VISIT www.theinsider.com/nyc

www.nytoday.com

0-595-29742-0